A BRAVE NEW SERIES

GLOBAL ISSUES IN A CHANGING WORLD

This new series of short, accessible think-pieces deals with leading global issues of relevance to humanity today. Intended for the enquiring reader and social activists in the North and the South, as well as students, the books explain what is at stake and question conventional ideas and policies. Drawn from many different parts of the world, the series' authors pay particular attention to the needs and interests of ordinary people, whether living in the rich industrial or the developing countries. They all share a common objective – to help stimulate new thinking and social action in the opening years of the new century.

Global Issues in a Changing World is a joint initiative by Zed Books in collaboration with a number of partner publishers and non-governmental organizations around the world. By working together, we intend to maximize the relevance and availability of the books published in the series.

PARTICIPATING NGOS

Both ENDS, Amsterdam
Catholic Institute for International Relations, London
Corner House, Sturminster Newton
Council on International and Public Affairs, New York
Dag Hammarskjöld Foundation, Uppsala
Development GAP, Washington DC
Focus on the Global South, Bangkok
Inter Pares, Ottawa
Public Interest Research Centre, Delhi
Third World Network, Penang
Third World Network–Africa, Accra
World Development Movement, London

ABOUT THIS SERIES

'Communities in the South are facing great difficulties in coping with global trends. I hope this brave new series will throw much needed light on the issues ahead and help us choose the right options.'

MARTIN KHOR, *Director,*
Third World Network, Penang

'There is no more important campaign than our struggle to bring the global economy under democratic control. But the issues are fearsomely complex. This Global Issues series is a valuable resource for the committed campaigner and the educated citizen.'

BARRY COATES, *Director,*
World Development Movement (WDM)

'Zed Books has long provided an inspiring list about the issues that touch and change people's lives. The Global Issues series is another dimension of Zed's fine record, allowing access to a range of subjects and authors that, to my knowledge, very few publishers have tried. I strongly recommend these new, powerful titles and this exciting series.'

JOHN PILGER, *author*

'We are all part of a generation that actually has the means to eliminate extreme poverty world-wide. Our task is to harness the forces of globalization for the benefit of working people, their families and their communities – that is our collective duty. The Global Issues series makes a powerful contribution to the global campaign for justice, sustainable and equitable development, and peaceful progress.'

GLENYS KINNOCK, MEP

ABOUT THE AUTHOR

HARRY SHUTT was educated at Oxford and Warwick universities. He worked for six years in the Development and Planning Division of the Economist Intelligence Unit (EIU). He then moved to the Research Department of the General and Municipal Workers' Union (1973–76) and subsequently became Chief Economist at the Fund for Research and Investment for the Development of Africa (1977–79). Since then he has been an independent economic consultant. His most recent book is *The Trouble with Capitalism: An Inquiry into the Causes of Global Economic Failure* (Zed Books, 1999). He is also the author of *The Myth of Free Trade: Patterns of Protectionism since 1945* (Basil Blackwell/The Economist, 1985).

Harry Shutt's *The Trouble with Capitalism*:
What the Critics Said

'Very stimulating.... Reads like an economics thriller.'
Business Economist

'Identifies an impressive array of potential problems.'
Christian Science Monitor

'One of the few to expose capitalism's lies and imperfections,
faults that critically threaten our democratic survival into
the next century.'
Publishers Weekly

'In this thoughtful treatment of the current economic scene,
one feels convinced by the end that the collapse of
Western civilization as we know it is at hand.'
Library Journal

'A timely book. Everyone who reads it will learn from it.
It is based on wide knowledge and sharp analysis.'
Libération

'Shutt [has] a message for every saver and investor:
a crash of 1929 proportions is almost inevitable.'
Guardian

'A powerful contribution to our understanding of the
problems with finance-led economic globalisation....
Even proponents of the dominant economic system
would do well to read this analysis.'
International Affairs

'The power and cogency of this work makes it a compelling
and deeply disturbing book: well written, well researched
and succinct.'
Chartist

A GLOBAL ISSUES TITLE

A NEW DEMOCRACY

Alternatives to a Bankrupt World Order

HARRY SHUTT

ZED BOOKS
London & New York

UNIVERSITY PRESS LTD
Dhaka

WHITE LOTUS CO. LTD
Bangkok

FERNWOOD PUBLISHING LTD
Halifax, Nova Scotia

DAVID PHILIP
Cape Town

BOOKS FOR CHANGE
Bangalore

A New Democracy: Alternatives to a Bankrupt World Order
was first published in 2001 by

In Bangladesh: The University Press Ltd, Red Crescent Building,
114, Motijheel C/A, PO Box 2611, Dhaka 1000

In Burma, Cambodia, Laos, Thailand and Vietnam:
White Lotus Co. Ltd, GPO Box 1141, Bangkok 10501, Thailand

In Canada: Fernwood Publishing Ltd, PO Box 9409, Station A,
Halifax, Nova Scotia, Canada B3K 5S3

In India: Books for Change, SKIP House,
25/1 Museum Road, Bangalore 560025

In Southern Africa: David Philip Publishers (Pty Ltd),
208 Werdmuller Centre, Claremont 7735, South Africa

In the rest of the world:
Zed Books Ltd, 7 Cynthia Street, London N1 9JF UK and
Room 400, 175 Fifth Avenue, New York, NY 10010, USA

Cover designed by Andrew Corbett
Designed and typeset in Monotype Bembo by Illuminati, Grosmont

A catalogue record for this book is available from the British Library

US CIP data is available from the Library of Congress

Canadian CIP data is available from the National Library of Canada

ISBN 1 55266 065 6 Pb. (Canada)

ISBN 0 86486 512 0 Pb. (Southern Africa)

ISBN 1 85649 973 1 Hb. (Zed Books)

ISBN 1 85649 974 x Pb. (Zed Books)

CONTENTS

BOXES

Acknowledgments

I wish to thank Garth Armstrong and Steve Pryle for their valuable comments and suggestions, which have resulted in significant improvements to the original manuscript. As always, however, final responsibility for both the views expressed and any surviving errors rests with the author.

BREAKDOWN OF THE WORLD ORDER

When the Berlin Wall fell in 1989, symbolically marking the end of the Cold War, there was a widespread surge of optimism in the world, as people looked forward to the prospect of freedom from the threat of world war and nuclear holocaust. This belief in the possibility of a 'new world order' was reinforced by the seeming outbreak of peace over the next few years in a number of long-standing regional conflicts, notably in Southern Africa and the Middle East. Moreover, the hope that turning swords into ploughshares could also herald a new era of global prosperity was strengthened in the eyes of many by the perception that the whole world could now benefit from adopting the market economy model in place of the failed system of Soviet central planning.

Even without the benefit of hindsight, however, it is possible to recognize that such optimism was always misplaced and that it ignored the existence of some growing global problems, which even then should have given world leaders cause for alarm. These included the crumbling of civil order in parts of the developing world and the former Soviet Union, the soaring numbers of people seeking asylum in western Europe and the US, and the emergence of a growing 'underclass' in many parts of the developed world arising from chronic high unemployment and rising poverty. Perhaps most disturbing of all should have been the bursting in 1990 of a speculative investment bubble in Japan (the world's second largest economy) from which neither its financial market nor the economy as a whole have ever shown any sign of recovering.

Yet for much of the intervening decade both official western propaganda and a generally complacent mass media dominated by big business interests have largely chosen to ignore or play down the significance of such indicators. On the contrary nearly all the most influential opinion formers have sought to emphasize the great economic benefits to be expected from the spread of 'globalization' – as more and more countries have been induced to open their borders to the free flow of goods, services and capital. Until the late 1990s the synthetic euphoria over this phenomenon even survived the successive financial crises which overtook one 'emerging' market after another (starting with Mexico in 1994). Moreover, just as the benefits of globalization were conclusively shown to be a mirage by the crises in East Asia and Russia in 1997–98,[1] the cheerleaders of 'free market' capitalism sought to conjure up an even more implausible fantasy. This was the idea of the 'new economy' – based on the application of micro-electronics and cyber-technology – which it was claimed would enable the United States and other countries embracing it permanently to break free from the shackles of the business cycle of boom and bust.

Meanwhile, in stark contrast to such wishful thinking, conditions in the real economy have inexorably deteriorated further. So far from globalization having reversed the declining fortunes of the Third World and the former Communist countries, it is seen to have exacerbated their plight by facilitating destabilizing inflows and outflows of capital, thus contributing to serious disruption in economic activity and the still wider spread of breakdown in civil authority in every continent. Likewise in the rich countries the condition of the large minority of the population who are economically marginalized is made still worse by decaying public services, which also now cause increasing distress to the middle class as well. Still more alarming for the latter is the looming prospect of a massive decline in their living standards as falling financial markets undermine the value of their pension funds.

This unfolding global economic disaster may be viewed at one level as merely the latest in a series of major downturns to have periodically afflicted the world economy since capitalism became the dominant mode of economic organization some 200 years ago. However, as this book will show, there is every reason to believe this one will prove the most cataclysmic ever, not least because official policy has been dedicated as never before to using the resources of the state to conceal or suppress the symptoms of economic imbalance and market failure.

Nevertheless, for all this official determination to maintain a Panglossian illusion of economic success, the recurrent financial crises since 1990 have inevitably caused doubts to creep in, particularly as stock market valuations have been driven to ever more fantastic (and wholly unprecedented) levels. Thus even some of the world's most respected financiers have begun to talk of the dangers of systemic financial crisis and of the vast over-inflation of the stock valuations of internet companies that have never made a profit.[2] Yet while a few such high priests of capitalism have felt moved to point out that the world could be close to the brink of an economic disaster worse than any since the 1930s, what none of them has been willing or able to do is propose any remedies that come close to addressing the fundamental problem.

For it is evident that the global establishment cannot contemplate any moves to bring about a more stable, less destructive economic order without fatally damaging its own position of immense wealth and power. This is because the essential features of any such reformed economic model would have to encompass: (i) measures greatly restricting the freedom of corporations to pursue maximization of their profits; and (ii) a substantial redistribution of income and wealth in favour of the presently deprived majority of the world's population. Equally, however, the ruling élite cannot willingly submit to the pitiless dictates of market forces for fear of a catastrophic diminution of its own wealth in the long postponed financial crisis.

Thus increasingly the world's leadership, firmly in thrall to corporate America, appears to resemble that of the doomed Soviet Union in its final phase. Unable to contemplate the drastic changes that are necessary to save the world from burgeoning catastrophe – or even any watering down of their outmoded ideology – they are reduced to a strategy of muddling through, in the hope that somehow the worst may yet be averted. Moreover, despite the much greater freedom of expression in the west than ever existed in the Soviet Union, western leaders still largely manage to shut themselves off from reality by surrounding themselves with advisers – and packing the media with commentators – who tell them nothing they do not want to hear.

Yet whatever the fantasies with which they seek to delude themselves and the public, world leaders are undoubtedly more conscious than ever of the need to neutralize popular discontent. For the growth and spread of democratic forces since the nineteenth century, however deficient their expression remains, has meant that in developed western countries at least it is no longer acceptable to allow the mass impoverishment of the population in order to try and preserve the capitalist profits system intact.

Just as important as these political realities in the industrialized west is the continuing spread of belief in the notion of universal human and democratic rights to all parts of the world. These principles have been enshrined in the basic documents of the United Nations since the 1940s. However, there is no doubt that the Cold War, continued over 40 years up to 1989, was used by the west as a very effective excuse for not demanding respect for human rights on the part of most of its allies in the 'free world'. This was justified on the grounds that it was not possible to play by the normal rules in the struggle against the Soviet enemy, which itself totally rejected such rules. Yet long before that conflict came to an end, the Carter administration in the United States (1977–81) had recognized this position as untenable, and by the start of the new century it has become politically very difficult, if not impossible, for the US openly to support authoritarian regimes anywhere.

Inevitably this pressure for the US finally to live up to its own rhetoric about freedom and democracy has seriously weakened its ability to impose its will on the world, even though now it has become the single, militarily unchallenged world superpower. In short it is being forced to come to terms with the long-recognized truth that imperialism is incompatible with democracy. The difficulty of resolving this dilemma is all the greater now that chaos and conflict induced by chronic economic failure are erupting in more and more regions of the world.

Hence the global establishment is having to confront the simultaneous breakdown both of the economic system which has ruled the world for the last two centuries and of the international political order, dominated by the US, which has been in place since 1945. It is being compelled to do so, moreover, against a background of manifestly unsustainable decay in the planet's natural environment – evidently associated with unprecedentedly rapid growth in the world's population and indiscriminate agricultural and industrial expansion over the last 100 years. This new challenge only serves to undermine even further a world order based on supposedly free market economic principles and on unilateral political control by one superpower.

This book is intended to contribute to filling the vacuum created by the refusal of the monolithic ruling establishment either to recognize the existence of fundamental weaknesses in the global status quo or to allow space for discussion of radically different models. It will be clear to the reader that the main purpose is to explore the alternative principles and approaches to economic and political organization that are needed to achieve a more stable and equitable world order. If it seems that this emphasis is somewhat at the expense of a fully adequate demonstration of why the present order is now becoming wholly unsustainable – at least in the economic sphere – it may be pointed out that:

- the body of published evidence and analysis pointing to this conclusion is by now already overwhelming, notwithstanding the zealous attempts of the mainstream media to ignore it;
- the space limitations imposed on the present work make it necessary to take certain assumptions as read.[3]

As will also be apparent, many of the new approaches identified as necessary are already starting to be applied by default, albeit with little official encouragement or publicity. As the global crisis intensifies in the wake of the now inevitable economic meltdown, the need for an open debate on how to construct a more functional global order has never been more pressing.

CHAPTER I

THE WANING OF IMPERIALISM

It is a striking fact that at the start of the twenty-first century the nature of the world order – in terms of the way that global power is exercised – is essentially the same as it was at the beginning of the last century. That is to say that the world is under the effective hegemony of the industrialized nations of North America and Europe (with Japan also having an associate role), which also broadly represent the interests of the world's most powerful private corporate entities, financial, commercial and industrial. This dominance has endured, it may be noted, in the face of cataclysmic upheavals during the intervening hundred years, including the two most destructive wars in history and the subsequent dissolution of the mainly European colonial empires which previously covered half the globe. Yet arguably the only major difference in the disposition of global power compared with a hundred years ago is that the United States has replaced Great Britain as the pre-eminent world power – and indeed is, at least superficially, in a far more unchallenged position of supremacy than Britain was in 1900.

Yet if such a quasi-imperialist world order has survived into the new century it is not for want of concerted efforts over the preceding hundred years – supported, at least rhetorically, by the imperialist powers themselves – to create a world order based on the explicit rejection of imperial domination of one country by another. Indeed the ideological movement against imperialism may be said to date back much further.

Arguably, in fact, this tendency has its origin in the ideas of individual liberty and intrinsic human equality that emerged from

6

the so-called Enlightenment of eighteenth-century Europe. By the beginning of the nineteenth century these beliefs had inspired not only the American and French revolutions but the start of a broader movement in Europe towards the suppression of the feudal practice of serfdom and the abolition of slavery throughout European colonial empires.[1] By the end of the nineteenth century this process had evolved into a spreading demand for the extension of political rights both in Europe and beyond, with such movements often taking a nationalist form.

Even before World War I the rise of national consciousness was associated, particularly in Europe, with the spread of representative democracy based on a steadily widening franchise. This trend had, for example, gradually made it impossible for Britain to resist the demand for Irish home rule, which was on the point of being finally accomplished in 1914 when it was forestalled by the outbreak of war. Likewise the United States felt obliged rapidly to concede the ultimate right of self-government to its newly acquired possession of the Philippines (seized from Spain in 1898). By 1918 President Wilson was moved to proclaim the principle of national self-determination as one of the main principles informing the Versailles peace treaties. However, it soon became apparent that this inherently ambiguous concept – which begs the question of what constitutes a nation – was only intended by the arbiters of the peace to apply to European states which had until then been under the sway of the now collapsed empires of Austria and Turkey. It is true that the principle that the interests and aspirations of the peoples of colonial territories must be taken into account by their rulers was implicit in the Covenant of the League of Nations. Yet it was obvious that the surviving imperial powers (principally Britain and France), which also turned out to be the dominant members of the League once the US Congress had voted to remain outside, were still far from prepared to accept the idea of self-determination unreservedly.

Thus for all the fine words of Wilson and the other founders of the League of Nations that body was never committed to the ending of colonial rule. However, with the outbreak of World War II, a far more definitive commitment to this principle was incorporated (at

the behest of the US) in the Atlantic Charter drawn up as a state-
ment of Anglo-American war aims,[2] and was subsequently enshrined
in the United Nations Charter at the end of the war. Thus already
by the middle of the century the ideology of imperialism which had
been so prevalent at its beginning had given way to official acceptance by the world's major powers that in principle all peoples had
the right to be governed in accordance with their freely expressed
wishes and that, by extension, colonial domination of one country
by another was no longer acceptable.

This change has had profound significance for the conduct of international relations ever since World War II – even though the ambigu-
ity of the concept of self-determination in a world where sovereignty
has continued to be vested in states which are seldom closely identified with 'nations' inevitably remains unresolved. This is because it
has imposed a need for any power exercising global hegemony to
maintain the position that it is doing so in the interests of preserving
or enhancing the 'freedom' of smaller nations – rather than, as in the
heyday of European imperialism, justifying colonial domination on
the basis of some supposed 'civilizing mission'. Indeed a familiar theory
among analysts of British imperial decline is that it was hastened by
the extension of democracy in Britain itself from the late nineteenth
century onwards, creating a progressively more glaring and morally
unacceptable contrast to the total denial of democracy in the colonies.[3] Furthermore, the notion that crude colonial domination was a
thing of the past had been reinforced by the acceptance that colonial
territories acquired by the victorious western allies as the spoils of
war in 1919 must be deemed to be held under the 'trusteeship' of the
League of Nations. Hence it seems to have been recognized even
then that there was an inherent contradiction between the very notion
of international hegemony exercised by a great power and the promotion of freedom or national self-determination.

Given this obvious tension, it is particularly ironic – in the light
of the history of the world since 1945 – that the leading champion
of the principle of self-determination and of opposition to colonialism
up to that time had been the United States. For it was this posture
which had enabled President Wilson to present his relatively young

country at the Versailles peace conference as the apostle of a new enlightened world order in which relations between countries would be governed in accordance with internationally agreed rules – in contrast to the narrow self-interest displayed by the old-established European powers such as Britain and France. Likewise, although Wilson's policy was thwarted by the isolationist tendencies which kept the US out of the League of Nations, even though he had been its leading architect, by the end of World War II the US was again able to appear as a relatively disinterested arbiter of the world's destiny – at least in the eyes of its European allies.

Yet precisely because from 1945 the United States was cast, or had cast itself, in the role of knight in shining armour to a world which had now formally espoused the right of national self-determination, it faced an implicit dilemma over how to exercise world hegemony now that it also found itself by far the most powerful nation on earth. The conundrum might well have seemed all the more awkward once the newly formed United Nations had adopted the Universal Declaration of Human Rights (with the support of the US and virtually all other member states barring the Soviet Union) in 1948. For if the old imperial powers of Europe had thus been forced to accept that their traditional style of colonial rule was a doomed anachronism, likewise the dominant power of the post-war world order now found itself the prisoner of its own rhetoric. In practice, as one of the leading State department policy makers of the time was forced to concede, the maintenance of US global dominance was not compatible with any claim to altruism and that consequently 'we should cease to talk about vague and ... unreal objectives such as human rights, the raising of living standards and democratisation'.[4]

THE ORIGINS AND NATURE OF PRESENT-DAY INTERNATIONAL INSTITUTIONS

This in-built contradiction in the post-World War II international order was manifest from the outset in the institutional structures that embodied it. Thus in keeping with the growing acceptance of the liberal democratic ideal in the west, the principles of both the sovereign equality of all nations and the equal right of all citizens to elect their governments were incorporated in the United Nations Charter in 1945 and the Universal Declaration of Human Rights (adopted by the UN in 1948). Yet throughout the subsequent half century, just as previously, there has never been any question but that global dominance was effectively concentrated in the hands of a small number of superpowers that wielded the greatest military force. Indeed the notion that some member states are more equal than others is implicit in the provision of the UN Charter that the five members with disproportionately more power (military or economic) should each be accorded permanent membership of the Security Council, giving them also a right of veto over any of the latter's resolutions. On the other hand, the UN Charter explicitly sanctifies the principle of non-interference by outside powers (or by the UN itself) in the internal affairs of any member state – in line with the presumption that national sovereignty is inviolable within a state's own territory.

The experience of the 50 years since the foundation of the UN has revealed even more glaring gaps between the actual conduct of international relations and the lofty sentiments of the UN Charter and the Universal Declaration of Human Rights than are in any case implicit in the ambiguities of the Charter itself. For not only have the great powers – and increasingly the US alone – come to dominate the decision-taking processes of the world body; the practical ability of most member states to assert their internal sovereignty has been chronically and conspicuously compromised. This anomalous situation stems from:

- the compelling *realpolitik* of geopolitical circumstances in which the distribution of power as between nation states has remained extremely uneven;
- the related huge imbalances in economic resources and living standards as between member states;
- prolonged distortions resulting from the Cold War;
- the failure to establish any remotely representative forms of democracy in the vast majority of UN member states, as well as the

persistent subversion of representative institutions even in the 'mature' democracies.

In fact, as noted above, the United States, which prior to 1945 had long posed as the champion of the international rule of law and the dismantling of colonial empires, recognized soon after World War II that as a newly established global superpower it could no longer afford to pay more than lip-service to such fine sentiments.[5] Indeed it is fair to say that any other country in the same position would probably have been forced to reach much the same conclusion in the circumstances prevailing in the post-war period. For the then prevailing world political climate was clearly not conducive to widespread adoption of the principles of sovereign equality and democracy. This was not only because the totalitarian Soviet Union and its satellites constituted a powerful negation of these ideals, but because nearly the whole of the rest of the world (apart from the Anglo-Saxon states and the majority of west European countries) was still under one form of authoritarian rule or another (many of them, indeed, still subject to the direct colonial control of the west European 'democracies').

RISE AND DECLINE OF THE COLD WAR

Another problem facing the United States after World War II was how to sustain the economic strength which was the basis of its power and the related prosperity which was vital to assuring the political consensus (both domestically and among its allies) in support of its superpower role. Undoubtedly the US leadership in 1945 was still painfully conscious of how fragile its own economy had proved between the wars and of the disastrous political consequences of such economic weakness both at home and (even more) abroad. It was also obviously aware that its full recovery from the Depression of the 1930s and the return to full employment had only been made possible by the outbreak of World War II and the opportunity this had given to US industry to become the 'arsenal of democracy'. Hence it was bound to be aware of the potentially negative economic impact of a sudden running down of the military machine and the massive defence industry once the war was over.

This consideration suggests strong *a priori* grounds for believing that there was always a high degree of ambivalence in the attitude of successive United States administrations toward its rivalry with the Soviet Union. For while the genuine antipathy on the part of the US leadership – and indeed of public opinion – to the possible spread of totalitarian Communism around the world can hardly be doubted, there are grounds for questioning whether such a threat was ever wholly credible – or would have been if the US and its allies had not so consistently aligned themselves with the forces of reaction in the Third World and elsewhere. For its part the Soviet Union seems also to have been substantially in thrall to its own military–industrial complex,[6] anxious to perpetuate its power and influence after the war. On the other hand there is also evidence that the Soviets, particularly in the early 1950s, were more willing to reach an accommodation in the Cold War than was the US.[7]

Yet however artificial the causes of the Cold War may have been, this conflict remained indisputably the dominant influence in international relations for at least 40 years after 1945. Thus virtually no issue in international affairs (or dispute between countries) during this period was unaffected by the rivalry between the two superpowers – even where, as for example in the Middle East, there was no inherent reflection of the rival communist and capitalist ideologies involved. Moreover many 'sovereign' nation states found that, willy-nilly, their domestic political affairs had become infected by the conflict and subverted by external forces linked to one side or the other. Not surprisingly, the tendency for this to happen was all the greater to the extent that the states involved controlled valuable economic resources or were considered to be otherwise of 'strategic' importance.

Thus in a rather obvious sense the Cold War, though presented by both the protagonists as a just struggle for freedom and against the forces of imperialist domination, was actually a convenient cover for each to pursue a global strategy of de facto imperialism. While clearly this did not entail overt colonial rule – and was more akin to the kind of indirect domination through client governments often practised by earlier imperial powers – it still amounted to a systematic negation of the principles of the UN Charter and the Universal Declaration of Human Rights. Although this contradiction presented a propaganda problem for both sides, it was inevitably a much greater one for the United States, which as leader of the 'free world' had to reconcile domestic public opinion (and among its allies) to this anomaly in a climate of far greater freedom of expression than ever prevailed in the Soviet bloc.

It has already been suggested that the US, whatever the natural inclinations of its rulers, had little choice in the aftermath of World War II but to adopt a quasi-imperial stance in pursuit of the attainment of global stability – a responsibility which it alone had the resources to fulfil. Yet if this made its adoption of such traditional *realpolitik* palatable to both domestic and (non-Soviet) world opinion for some time after the war, it was perhaps inevitable that the contrast between this approach and the idealistic rhetoric of western propaganda – enshrined in the founding documents of the UN – should progressively seem less tenable. Thus with the passing of time it became less and less acceptable that the US should assume the right to promote the overthrow of governments in countries from Guatemala to Greece on the pretext that this was necessary to contain Soviet expansionism – when in reality the reason for such subversion was that the governments concerned were deemed insufficiently amenable to US commercial and political interests. In other words, it was impossible to disguise the fact that the US was acting more in the manner of an old-fashioned imperial power rather than as the guardian of the 'free world'.

Precisely how or why this change of perception came about is debatable. It would certainly be simplistic, if comforting, to suggest that it reflected a growing revulsion (both at home and abroad) at US official hypocrisy. Almost certainly, however, world opinion found it progressively harder to believe in the reality of the 'red menace', as the Soviet Union showed little sign of posing a serious danger to the west after the Cuban missile crisis of 1962, until by the time it stumbled into the quagmire of the Afghan war at the end of the

1970s it had lost all credibility as a threat to global peace – except in the minds of die-hard cold warriors in Washington. Moreover, for American opinion in particular the Vietnam war (with its 58,000 US casualties) raised the question of whether its people were really willing to pay any price in defence of 'liberty', as President Kennedy had claimed, particularly where it was hard to see any vital US interests at stake.

Reaction to the Vietnam débâcle, combined with widespread domestic repugnance at the murderous excesses of a number of foreign military dictatorships backed by the US (notably in Latin America) in the 1970s, paved the way for the Carter administration's attempt (1977–81) to put more emphasis on promotion of human rights in foreign policy. Although this was followed by a reversion to cruder bullying tactics under the Reagan–Bush regime (Nicaragua, Grenada, Panama), it is notable that the administration felt constrained by fear of public opinion to make some effort to cover up its subversive activities, as in the Iran–Contra affair in Nicaragua. Moreover, it seems likely that Nicaragua's successful prosecution of the United States in the International Court of Justice in 1984 for making undeclared war[8] forced the US to realize there were potential limits to its ability to break international law in pursuit of foreign policy goals – even though the administration felt able to deny the ICJ's jurisdiction and ignore the judgement.

If such displays of naked hegemonic power were ceasing to be acceptable even while the Cold War was continuing, it was inevitable that they should be seen as even less so once the US–Soviet conflict had come to an end. This development, which was signalled almost as soon as Mikhail Gorbachev assumed the Soviet presidency in 1985 and was completed with the fall of the Berlin Wall in 1989, amounted to a declaration by Moscow that it was neither willing nor able to continue playing the game. Although the Reagan administration was to claim credit for having brought the 'evil empire' to its knees through its hard-line approach and intensification of the arms race in the early 1980s, there is no doubt that this sudden capitulation took the US by surprise – evidently because the CIA had failed to appreciate the extent of Soviet economic collapse. Hence Washington's immediate response to this dramatic change was confused, and its subsequent failure to formulate a coherent, realistic strategy for stabilizing post-Soviet Russia and its sister republics suggests considerable ambivalence towards the west's 'victory'.

POST-COLD WAR TENSIONS
(HEGEMONY VERSUS DEMOCRACY)

But whether or not US policy makers would have secretly preferred the Cold War to continue – thereby perpetuating what many of them doubtless still saw as a convenient justification for US intervention in other countries' affairs – its passing has unquestionably increased the pressure on them to try a more subtle approach. As will be argued in subsequent chapters, other forces are also pushing in this direction, not least the increasingly obvious failure of the economic strategies promoted by the US in its client states in the Third World and elsewhere – and typically imposed by distinctly authoritarian governments with little more than a veneer of democratic legitimacy.

There are, it is true, signs that Washington is searching for an alternative bogeyman with which to frighten the world community into at least tacit acceptance of continuing unilateral, extra-legal US intervention in the affairs of sovereign states. The most obvious candidate for this role to date has been the phenomenon identified in the western media as Islamic 'fundamentalism'. This may indeed seem a logical response to the fact that many groups identified with Islam have in recent years inspired violent resistance to the established order in different countries and regions of Asia, Africa and even Europe – and have generally been only too willing to identify themselves as leaders of a *jihad* (holy war) against US influence. It might also appeal to extreme supporters of Israel – arguably the world's only surviving exponent of traditional imperialism – of whom the most powerful are in the United States. Yet a moment's reflection must lead to the conclusion that any attempt by the US to launch a global crusade against this tendency comparable to the Cold War struggle against Communism would be fraught with serious peril.[9] For it would run the obvious risk of appearing to encourage religious (if not racial) discrimination – in defiance not only of the Universal Declaration of Human Rights but even of the US constitution – in a world where fine distinctions between the political aims of different Muslim sects would be hard to draw in propaganda terms. As such it would also risk antagonizing some traditional allies of the US such as Saudi Arabia and the other Gulf states, while at the same time serving to confirm the image of the United States as the 'Great Satan' in the eyes of all opponents of the still numerous repressive and reactionary regimes in the Islamic world. At the same time it clearly could never be a credible explanation of militant resistance to US domination in the extensive regions of the world (notably Latin America) which remain wholly untouched by Islam.

Hence successive administrations in Washington have thus far resisted any temptation to take up the challenge of 'holy war'. Instead they have been unable to come up with any clearer formulation of the common enemy of the international community than that of 'terrorism' in general. Yet the obvious problem with attempting to build a crusade against this undoubtedly widespread phenomenon is that there is universal awareness that terrorist activities occur all round the world in pursuit of a wide variety of causes, many of them supported (covertly or otherwise) by the United States or its client states. It is also well understood that terrorism often occurs either in response to or in support of the illegitimate exercise of political power – i.e. where there is little or no semblance of democratic expression or the rule of law. Such realities have not, however, inhibited the US from both selectively blacklisting certain 'terrorist states' – which it has sought to subject to international economic sanctions – and resorting to extra-legal methods to counter those terrorist movements defined as hostile to US interests, as in the bombing raid against a chemical factory in Sudan in 1998 in retaliation for bomb attacks on the US embassies in Kenya and Tanzania.

At the same time it is striking that, alone among major western governments, the Clinton administration, with full congressional backing, refused to support the creation of the International Criminal

Court when a large majority of UN member states voted to establish
it in 1998. This body, which is due to become operational once 60
member states have ratified the statute, will for the first time provide
a permanent mechanism[10] enabling the international community to
prosecute individuals suspected of war crimes, major human rights
abuses – and probably in due course acts of terrorism and aggression
– where it is deemed that the relevant national jurisdiction is unable
or unwilling to do so.[11] The US decision to oppose this innovation is
clearly significant, although one may doubt whether the official
reason for it – the fear that US peacekeeping personnel might be
arraigned by the Court – fully accounts for their decision to vote
against. For it is easy to see that such a major extension of the
international rule of law would tend to limit the scope for continuing
US unilateralism in identifying and pursuing international criminals,
applying criteria of arbitrary selectiveness determined solely by
'United States interests'.

There is thus plenty of evidence that, over ten years after the end
of its rivalry with the Soviet Union, the US still hankers after the
simple certainties of its hegemonic heyday in the 'bipolar' era. Yet
perhaps the most striking political reality of the era which has suc-
ceeded the Cold War is the ever more compelling need for world
leaders to take a clear stand in favour of democracy and against
authoritarian regimes of all kinds. This has forced Washington quite
abruptly to abandon once-favoured leaders such as Mobutu of Zaire
(now the Democratic Republic of Congo) and Suharto of Indonesia
as soon as they were seriously challenged from within, and has led it
to maintain a deafening silence over attempts to put ex-President
Pinochet of Chile (once a prominent US client in Latin America) on
trial for humanitarian crimes. Moreover the US administration has
generally been quick to denounce or warn against any coups in
opposition to elected governments and has maintained pressure on
such military juntas as have seized power to restore democracy as
soon as possible.

On the other hand it is noticeable that the US government has
made little serious effort to promote the removal of undemocratic
regimes which are still more or less strongly entrenched, especially

where it perceives its national economic or political interests to be best served by tacitly supporting the status quo. This has been most conspicuously true in the Middle East, where governments have remained almost uniformly authoritarian since the end of the Cold War without any apparent objection from the US. Indeed, when the Bush administration was presented with the opportunity to help over-throw tyranny and establish democracy in Iraq at the end of the Gulf War in 1991 it pointedly declined to do so. It also gave tacit support to the suppression of the democratic process by the military in Algeria in 1992, inaugurating a prolonged period of bloodshed and repression. In a similar spirit neither the Clinton administration nor its successor has to date shown much inclination to encourage the forces of liberal democracy which have begun to appear in Iran since the late 1990s, preferring to continue demonizing the country as a terrorist state. Meanwhile the medieval autocracies of Saudi Arabia and the Gulf states remain above official US criticism. Indeed there are obvious grounds for supposing that US tolerance of continuing authoritarianism in the Middle East region has been maintained primarily out of a desire to humour the rulers of these oil-rich countries. The latter's paranoid fear of any kind of political liberalism was well demonstrated by Saudi Arabia's ferocious hostility to the attempt to hold more or less open, multi-party elections in the neighbouring state of Yemen in 1993, while there can be little doubt that the same syndrome has been a major factor behind the allies' refusal to give meaningful support to democratic forces in either Iraq or Kuwait since the Gulf War.

While concern to preserve its security of access to the world's major oil reserves is clearly an important motivation for Washington's support for anti-democratic tendencies in the Middle East, it is not the only explanation. Another powerful influence on the attitude of successive US administrations to Middle Eastern politics has been the Palestine question – the central diplomatic issue of the region for the past fifty years – on which the Zionist lobby has been extremely effective in assuring unwavering presidential and congressional support for Israel. In this context there can be little doubt that both the US and Israel have preferred to deal with autocratic Arab governments, both because these have been easier to pressurize towards compromise with Israel – in the face of overwhelming popular hostility to the latter in the Arab world – and because it may seem useful propaganda to be able to contrast 'democratic' Israel with authoritarian Arab states.

But perhaps the most conspicuous betrayal by the US government of its own professed commitment to upholding democracy and human rights in the post-Cold War world has been in relation to the People's Republic of China. This is all the more striking in view of both the latter's high profile abuses (notably the Tiananmen Square massacre in Beijing in 1989) and the powerful rhetoric denouncing them emanating equally from Congress and from President Clinton himself, particularly when he was first running for office in 1992. It is of course quite understandable, in terms of traditional great power *realpolitik*, that a large and important state (in both military and economic terms) such as China should be treated with greater deference than countries such as Burma, Sudan or Cuba. Yet inevitably, in an age when the world's sole superpower feels it must purport to uphold an internationally established code of human rights, such blatant and sustained inconsistency tends to undermine international respect for its foreign policy and give encouragement to the many actual and aspiring national leaders round the world who seek to revalidate the traditional precept that 'might is right'.

It is because the US government is conscious of this contradiction – and of the unacceptability, not least in the eyes of the public at home, of reverting to the cruder methods of subversion it employed in the heyday of the Cold War – that it is now constrained to follow slightly more subtle approaches to gaining its ends. Thus it has become increasingly accustomed since the 1980s to put pressure on governments in the Third World and the former Soviet bloc by means of de facto economic sanctions, or the threat of them. These commonly take the form of restricting access to official development aid or loan finance, typically with the connivance of the International Monetary Fund or the World Bank, the dominant multilateral aid agencies, which are effectively controlled by the US. Such tactics are combined with more traditional instruments of subversion, such as offering material and propaganda support to a favoured party within the 'democratic' process of individual states and the usual panoply of bribes to political leaders in return for their support for US interests. As such they form a continuum with the neo-imperialist strategy of manipulating Third World and other states which has been followed by the US, often in collusion with Britain, France and other former colonial powers, ever since decolonization took place (primarily in the 1950s and 1960s) – and indeed is strongly reminiscent of the pattern of 'indirect rule' which was such a characteristic feature of British administration in India and elsewhere.

By now, however, it is becoming more and more widely perceived that this approach to maintaining hegemony is ultimately no more sustainable than crude military subversion, for a number of related reasons, namely:

1. Where policy changes are seen to be imposed on a national government from outside they inevitably tend to undermine the legitimacy of the very process of government, whether the country concerned practises nominal democratic accountability or not. Thus the buying of policy 'reform' with aid funds comes to be viewed as just a form of institutionalized extortion or bribery, which not only corrupts the principal actors but engenders increasing popular cynicism and contempt for the whole system.
2. Since the imposed policies are themselves all too often shown to be hopelessly unrealistic and damaging to the economy and to living standards, to the extent that they can be implemented at all, their effect is to intensify popular discontent.
3. In such a climate of corruption and alienation it is all too common to find that the integrity and effectiveness of institutions and administrations progressively breaks down.

This deteriorating social and political environment is, moreover, being compounded by chronic global economic slowdown and financial instability – the full significance of which is examined in the next chapter. The inevitable outcome is a rising incidence of breakdown in civil order, and in more and more cases a slide into actual war, both within and between states. Since the early 1990s the latter has become a particularly widespread phenomenon in Africa, with the number of ongoing wars on that continent having at least doubled (to twelve or more) in the subsequent ten years – notwithstanding the ending of the Cold War and of the apartheid regime in South Africa, which led to the end of conflict in Mozambique and Namibia (though not in Angola). Yet manifestly no continent is exempt from this trend, with an ever-rising incidence of rebellion and secession in Latin America (including large and relatively wealthy countries such as Colombia and Mexico), Asia (Afghanistan, Indonesia, the Philippines and Sri Lanka), the former Soviet bloc (the Balkans, Chechnya, Central Asia and Transcaucasia) and latterly even the South Pacific (Fiji and the Solomon Islands). It would, of course, be simplistic to suggest that all these conflicts have identical causes – or even that the primary factor involved is necessarily the heavy-handed attempt of the US to manipulate the governments concerned in defiance of popular aspirations. It is nevertheless clear that it is becoming impossible to address or suppress the increasingly complex and urgent problems of the world by the imposition of a *Pax Americana* driven by a narrow and self-serving interpretation of US interests.

Nor is this to suggest that the United States could or should strive to develop a more enlightened strategy towards the world such as to render its hegemony more acceptable and effective. Rather the conclusion to be drawn is the not very original one that a civilization that purports to be based on the twin pillars of democracy and the rule of law cannot for long impose itself on the rest of the world by systematically betraying these principles. It should be apparent, moreover, that this is not simply a question of moral consistency and political credibility. For both contemporary experience and past history demonstrate that any attempt to sustain an empire based on unrepresentative, authoritarian institutions must ultimately fail because of the imperial power's inherent inability either to understand or adequately respond to changing circumstances and popular pressures, thereby ensuring its own downfall. Moreover, whereas earlier empires (such as that of Rome) might survive such weaknesses for centuries, in the contemporary world they arguably cannot long withstand the pressures stemming from rising expectations and much greater public awareness based on mass literacy and rapid communications.

We have thus in a sense been brought full circle: to a rather trite confirmation of the central criticism of traditional imperialism earlier in the twentieth century – that it is simply incompatible with any interpretation of the principles of liberal democracy. Yet if such a conclusion is not new it is nevertheless worth recollecting that the attempt to apply such principles to the conduct of world affairs over the past hundred years – however inconsistently – is revolutionary in terms of what went before. It follows that, in considering how international relations might evolve henceforth, we must depart from the type of traditional historical analysis which treats them in terms of the secular rise and fall of empires or of attempts to maintain a balance of power between the dominant states in the tradition of Metternich and other nineteenth-century statesmen.[12] For in an age of greater democracy – albeit still quite primitive even in the 'advanced' countries – it is arguably inevitable that quasi-imperial powers will feel constrained not only to view the traditional concepts of empire and absolutist *realpolitik* with growing disdain but to make a more far-sighted calculation of their own national economic interests.

The ability of the US (with the connivance of its allies) to perpetuate a contradictory juxtaposition of neo-imperialism and promotion of liberal democracy in the post-World War II era was, as suggested earlier, only made possible by the Cold War. With the passing of that conflict not only is the United States being forced to confront the ever more stark hypocrisy of its own approach to dominating the globe; it is having to do so against the background of an economic order which is showing symptoms of greater instability and destructiveness than at any time in its history.

CHAPTER 2

CAPITALIST CRISIS
AND THE THREAT TO
US HEGEMONY

Just as the spread of belief in universal human rights and democracy since the eighteenth century has rendered the practice of imperialism progressively less acceptable, so it has also gradually made less tolerable the extreme material deprivation of substantial sections of the population, at least in those industrialized countries where representative government has become established. In fact it is ironic that it was the rise of industrial capitalism, itself also a product of the eighteenth-century Enlightenment, which was to create such unprecedented extremes of poverty and destitution in nineteenth-century Europe as to provoke previously unheard of levels of resistance from the poor themselves.

For whereas the political ideas associated with the Enlightenment heralded the liberation of European society from the constricting traditions of feudalism and religious obscurantism, it was soon found that in the economic sphere such liberalism was to exact a heavy price from the working masses. For not only were huge numbers of people uprooted from their traditional rural existence by a combination of the Agricultural Revolution (which deprived them of land) and the Industrial Revolution, which pushed them into new and unhealthy urban environments; it also subjected them to even greater economic insecurity than they had previously endured under feudalism. This was because of the phenomenon known as the business cycle, which under *laissez-faire* capitalism resulted in a chronic tendency to excess investment and output, inevitably ensuring that boom was followed by bust in one product market after another. While such instability had also affected the largely rural pre-capitalist economy, the resulting economic and social deprivation under the quasi-feudal society that had previously prevailed was generally less severe in the absence of a strong compulsion on landowners to push their tenants into destitution in order to maximize profits. Under capitalism, how-ever, the logic of the market had to be ruthlessly applied, resulting in recurrent and widespread social misery in nineteenth-century Europe.

Although these economically marginalized classes were excluded from the political process for much of the nineteenth century – when voting rights were still confined to those with at least a modicum of wealth – it was soon recognized that the resulting degra-dation of large segments of the population was not tolerable. The consequent pressures for change, culminating in the outbreak of revo-lutionary movements across continental Europe in 1848 in response to a generalized economic slump, made concessions inevitable. Fear-ing the threat of further such movements, the ruling bourgeois élites felt obliged (by the end of the century) to concede not only a progressive extension of voting rights to the working masses but an increasing range of welfare benefits, including old-age pensions, un-employment insurance and free elementary education.

Yet these systems were subsequently overwhelmed by the great depression of the 1930s, when the huge numbers of unemployed far outstripped the resources available to pay adequate benefits. The re-sulting widespread social misery was a major factor behind the rise of Fascism and Nazism, leading to the outbreak of World War II. Hence by the end of the war policy makers everywhere had resolved that it should never be allowed to happen again. They accepted that it must henceforth be the primary objective of economic policy to assure full employment and to apply whatever level of state interven-tion was needed to achieve this – in line with the economic theories developed by J.M. Keynes – while continuing to provide an ad-equate social safety net for those unable to work.

ORIGINS AND DECLINE OF THE POST-WAR BOOM

In the event, for some 25 years after World War II the international economy developed in a way that seemed to vindicate Keynesian strategies and thus to suggest that capitalism could after all be made compatible with long-term economic and social stability. Equally, its post-war development was for a long time entirely satisfactory from the perspective of US corporate and geo-political interests. Not only did it grow at a faster rate than in any comparable period since the Industrial Revolution, both the flow of US capital to other countries and international trade in goods and services were greatly facilitated. At the same time the defence expenditure necessitated by the Cold War provided the scope for continuing expansion by the military-industrial complex, which would otherwise have suffered serious negative consequences from post-war cutbacks. All the while, of course, the anti-Soviet struggle also provided cover for selective military interventions and subversion of foreign governments deemed hostile to US commercial interests – notably in Latin America – even where there was no obvious threat to world peace.

As long as this climate of seemingly effortless global expansion persisted the consolidation of US hegemony – economic, military and political – in the 'free world' proceeded without serious challenge, underpinned by a widespread sense of increasing prosperity. However, once the long post-war boom came to an end in the early 1970s, the economic climate favouring both the Keynesian model of capitalism and the global expansion of corporate America started to deteriorate and has continued to do so ever since. The main symptoms of this long-term weakening, which have inevitably spilt over from the developed market economies to the poorer Third World countries, have been fourfold.

Declining economic growth rates From a peak of over 5 per cent a year attained in the 1960–73 period, the average growth rate of the world economy (i.e. of its aggregate Gross Domestic Product) has progressively declined, from one decade to the next, to an average of barely more than 2 per cent a year recorded in the 1990s.[1] (It should be noted that this reality has been largely obscured from public view by official propaganda insistent on emphasizing the positive within the overall picture: first the phenomenal East Asian growth of the 1970s and 1980s, and then, as the latter faded, the sustained, credit-fuelled US boom of the 1990s). While the reasons for this chronic deterioration are complex and debatable, it almost certainly represents a return to more-or-less normal rates of growth after the exceptional expansion of the post-war boom that lasted up to the early 1970s. With the benefit of hindsight it is now possible to see that this boom was largely a response to the huge economic stimulus provided by the unprecedented destruction of World War II. Yet whatever the precise explanation for the prolonged downward trend of the last three decades, it has undoubtedly given the lie to the optimistic post-war belief among most western economists that the key to assuring perpetual rapid growth – in the shape of Keynesian policies of demand management – had been discovered. On the contrary, it is now clear that the traditional business cycle of boom and bust is ultimately as inescapable as ever.

Intensifying competition for markets and shrinking outlets for investment As in earlier prolonged economic downturns of the capitalist era, the response of private businesses has been to try and sharpen their competitive edge so as to maintain or increase their share of more slowly growing markets and thus the rate of return on their assets employed. This has entailed efforts to increase the efficiency of their operations, with particular emphasis on raising the productivity of labour and capital. Against a background of continuing relative stagnation of global demand this has inevitably led to a squeeze on corporate profits, a shakeout of labour and a slowdown in the growth of fixed capital investment. The consequent 'vanishing of investment opportunity',[2] moreover, inevitably brought with it the classic threat to the stability of the whole system – by weakening the demand for capital itself and thus tending to undermine the value of financial securities and investment funds. (It should of course be stressed that there has never been any shortage of demand for capital to invest in public infrastructure, such as schools and hospitals, or in productive enterprise in the Third World, but that this could not normally offer rates of return that are high enough relative to perceived risk to be attractive to western financiers.)

Rising unemployment and public indebtedness The labour market shakeout has in turn precipitated a rise in unemployment throughout the industrialized world (the OECD[3] countries) from the ratios of 2 to 3 per cent of the labour force they typically enjoyed up to the early 1970s to 8 per cent or more in the 1980s and 1990s. As a result rates of pay (particularly among the less skilled) have been squeezed and claims for unemployment and other social security benefits from the increasing numbers of deprived citizens – under the relatively generous welfare systems designed in these countries in the post-war era – have ballooned to barely sustainable levels. Despite extensive moves to reduce entitlements under these schemes, the cumulative effect of slowing growth and rising unemployment, combined with pressures to cut taxes so as to sustain the profitability of the corporate sector, over the last quarter of the twentieth century has been to push all the industrialized countries into chronic budgetary deficit. The result has been that the gross public sector debt of the OECD countries more than doubled as a proportion of national income between 1975 and 2000 (to over 70 per cent).

Recurrent inflation and increased currency instability The effort of governments to sustain and revive growth – by holding down interest rates and running chronic budget deficits – was also reflected in recurring bouts of high inflation from the 1970s. This in turn fed quite rapid currency devaluation, in contrast to the general stability of exchange rates in the post-war era. This tendency was given great impetus by the US decision to abandon the fixed parity of the dollar against gold in 1971, thereby ending the global monetary regime established at Bretton Woods at the end of World War II. While it is true, at the time of writing, that there has been no major outbreak of global inflation since the early 1990s, the fear that it may recur – and that currency parities may suddenly change – remains a significant destabilizing factor in the global economy.

THE RESPONSE TO PROLONGED DOWNTURN

Despite initial optimism that the unfavourable trends which began in the 1970s would be short-lived, and that the pattern of rapid growth would be resumed, successive efforts to bring about a sustained recovery over the subsequent 25 years have proved vain. At the same time, however, there has never been any question of accepting the traditional logic of the capitalist business cycle, requiring a severe and perhaps prolonged shakeout of global productive capacity – and a corresponding slump in the market value of securities. Such resistance to market forces has been driven by two very powerful and related motives, namely:

- Fear of the political consequences of such a slump, bearing in mind the fall in living standards that would be bound to result. Such an outcome, be it noted, would be felt not only through the curtailment of welfare benefits which the state would no longer be able to afford, but also through the collapse of the large number of privately funded pension schemes. For the sustainability of such schemes – which did not exist at the time of earlier economic slumps such as that of the 1930s – is contingent on a more or less perpetually rising stock market.
- The desire of big business to avoid major financial losses and corporate collapses which would also result from a severe or prolonged fall in the stock market. This has doubtless been all the greater to the extent that the potential level of resulting bad debts was, even by the early 1970s, still higher than that which had wreaked such havoc in the 1930s. Moreover, the governments which had promoted this profligacy by underwriting private sector debt as 'lenders of last resort' would be unable to bail out all the losers in the event of a systemic financial failure, while at the same time meeting all their other budgetary obligations.

But if the idea of submitting to the traditional capitalist medicine of sustained depression was considered no longer tenable, so also, it was tacitly concluded by the end of the 1970s, was the post-war consensus based on the sanctity of the welfare state providing universal benefits for those in need. In fact it had never been envisaged that this structure would need to withstand the strain of chronic high unemployment.[4] For once unemployment rates had become obstinately stabilized at 7–8 per cent of the working population and the prospect of renewed rapid growth had receded, the resulting rise in state budget deficits and debt in the developed market economies was seen to be unsustainable.

From this stark conclusion it inevitably followed that the only politically acceptable route to economic survival was one involving a steadily intensifying squeeze on most forms of public expenditure, particularly on entitlements to and levels of social welfare benefits. Yet this was not by itself sufficient to resolve the central problem created by chronic economic stagnation (from the standpoint of the US and the world capitalist establishment): the inadequate level of corporate profits. Hence it was found necessary to use state fiscal policy to confer more and more benefits on the private business sector and on investors, both through tax breaks and various forms of de facto subsidization of profits – or 'corporate welfare' – while yet pretending that the key to economic success was to curb state intervention.

It was also perceived as essential to reduce or eliminate remaining restraints on cross-border movements of capital, goods and services, thereby severely restricting governments' ability to tax or otherwise curb profits – while simultaneously enabling investors to pursue the most profitable opportunities anywhere in the world. At the same time restraints on financial markets and institutions, imposed in the 1930s in order to prevent a recurrence of the devastating abuses of that period, began to be removed in the hope of providing further stimulus to investment. Likewise, under the guise of 'rolling back the frontiers of the state', there was from the early 1980s a growing worldwide trend – pioneered by the Thatcher government in Britain – towards privatization of state-owned enterprises, ostensibly designed to reduce the burden borne by taxpayers but actually to provide an outlet for the excessive amounts of private capital for which there was otherwise diminishing demand.[5] The justification for this strategy was, moreover, given artificial plausibility by cuts in taxation – designed principally to boost corporate profits – thereby reducing state funds available for investment in public utilities, which, it could then be claimed, might be financed only by the private sector. Thus the state was mobilized both to sustain the necessary perpetual expansion of capitalist profits and to provide new outlets for the recycling of those otherwise redundant profits.

STRUGGLING TO CONTAIN THE GLOBAL CRISIS

As should have been expected in the light of past experience, this experiment in pseudo-*laissez-faire* economics was doomed to failure from the outset. Thus even by the beginning of the 1990s any hopes that such attempts to rekindle the spirit of enterprise could provide a lasting boost to global growth were demolished by a financial crisis (triggered by the collapse of a worldwide speculative real estate boom)[6] and renewed recession. This setback might have had more severe political consequences but for the fact that it coincided with the final collapse of the even more discredited Soviet system, which enabled propagandists for free market capitalism to proclaim its ultimate triumph and even pretend that the 'end of history' had arrived.

In the subsequent decade recovery has been limited and fitful, as the effort to avert financial catastrophe has entailed resorting to increasingly desperate measures, mainly designed to avert a collapse in the market value of shares and other securities – notwithstanding an increasingly bleak economic outlook. Such expedients have included:

- The use of ever greater tax incentives to investment so as to boost the demand for shares and other financial securities and thereby sustain their market prices. This has involved encouraging the further expansion of funded pension schemes – established in the US since the 1950s – which many company employees have been effectively coerced into joining (by making their contributions tax deductible). This is happening, moreover, at a time when it is becoming manifestly impossible to guarantee proper pension levels for those scheme members entering retirement – as the flow of funds into the market has inflated the value of securities against a background of shrinking scope for boosting profits. This has been reflected since the early 1990s in the steady switch of company pension schemes away from offering pensions guaranteed to be a fixed proportion of employees' final salary to ones which give no certainty as to their final value, leaving pensioners entirely at the mercy of fluctuating financial markets. Meanwhile belief in the need to perpetuate this ruinous system is being sustained by the transparently fraudulent notion that the proportion of retired

people in the population is growing to the point where it can no
longer be borne by state-run pay-as-you-go systems (based on a
combination of contributions from those in work and transfers
from general taxation).[7]

- Progressively greater relaxation of controls on financial markets
  such as to invite manipulation of the market value of assets and
  even outright fraud. Thus, for example, starting in the US around
  1980, companies in most OECD countries have been permitted
  to buy back their own shares (outlawed in the 1930s), while more
  and more companies which have never made a profit have been
  allowed to have their shares traded on stock exchanges. At the same
  time companies, their auditors and analysts advising investors
  (whose supposed objectivity is increasingly compromised by conflicts of interest) have enjoyed great latitude in presenting company financial data to the public in an unduly favourable light.

The difficulties of thus artificially sustaining the value of capital
have intensified since the early 1990s, although this has been little
appreciated by the public at large, or even by most investors, beguiled
by the incessant corporate and media 'hard sell' of the globalized, hi-
tech economic miracle. In Japan, by contrast, neither investor confidence nor the real economy has ever recovered from the stock market
crash of 1990, so that by early 2001 the main Tokyo share index was
languishing at barely one-third of its peak of 11 years earlier. Likewise 'emerging' markets in Asia and Latin America, which in the
early 1990s had been proclaimed as the brightest investment prospect
of the twenty-first century, have suffered successive financial crises
from which they show little sign of recovering – notwithstanding
the determination of many investors, as well as the IMF, to pretend
otherwise. Meanwhile in the industrialized west recovery has only
been sustained by still greater financial liberalization and officially
encouraged speculative excess, particularly in the United States.

Thus since the early 1980s banks have been given ever greater
latitude to expand their lending (i.e. effectively to print money)
more or less indiscriminately, in the confident expectation that the
taxpayer will bail them out in the event of major default, particularly
where institutions are considered 'too big to fail'. Yet perhaps the

defining spectacle of this surreal economic climate was that of Alan Greenspan, Chairman of the Federal Reserve Board (the US central bank), lending his support to a manifestly nonsensical theory in order to explain the phenomenal rise in the US stock market after 1994 – which by early 2000 had caused the average prices of shares to reach multiples of earnings far higher even than those recorded before the Wall Street Crash of 1929. According to this so-called 'new economy' theory this boom was justified by the supposedly unprecedented growth of US productive potential caused by the application of information technology, thus in turn enabling the economy to grow at much higher rates without causing inflation. Equally astonishing was the unwillingness of the vast majority of admiring congressmen and analysts to point out the obvious flaws in this absurd notion, particularly its failure to take any account of the problem of deficient demand, the real constraint to higher growth – as was to be demonstrated when the sales of most leading technology companies collapsed suddenly at the end of 2000.[8]

An equally graphic demonstration of this refusal to recognize the central importance of global excess capacity relative to weak effective demand is reflected in the mainstream analysis of the chronic stagnation that has afflicted the Japanese economy since the early 1990s. For the bulk of western (and Japanese) economic opinion has held that this phenomenon – reflected in a decline in annual GDP growth from a world-beating average of over 6 per cent in the 30 years to 1991 to under 1 per cent in the subsequent 10 years – is largely the result of the country's failure to enforce market discipline (requiring mass bankruptcy of failed businesses) in the wake of the stock market crash of 1990. It is certainly true that the continuing overhang of bad debts has had a depressive effect on the domestic economy. Yet the most fundamental impediment to recovery has unquestionably been the weakness of demand – and intensifying competition – in the export markets which had provided the main basis for fast Japanese growth in earlier decades. What has been hard to admit, both for Japanese leaders and their American patrons, is that Japan's earlier strategy of expansion through taking a disproportionately large share of world markets for a vast range of products, from automobiles to video recorders, was bound to prove unsustainable. In fact this strategy (which was buttressed by a degree of orchestrated government support unknown in other industrialized countries – but also tacitly encouraged by the US in pursuit of its Cold War global strategy) was bound to meet increasing resistance from other countries as the world economy became progressively more stagnant – and as new competitors (notably China) were also boosting global over-capacity still further. Hence it served to endow Japan with an economic structure that was seriously distorted and unbalanced, being excessively oriented to supplying export markets no longer able to absorb its excess output but ill-equipped to supply its heavily protected domestic market with most goods and services at competitive prices.

These intensifying distortions and contradictions are symptomatic of the growing difficulty of maintaining the belief that there is a long-term remedy for capitalism's systemic weakness, particularly one that may be compatible with tolerable social conditions. A more fundamental but unavoidable inconsistency in the agenda of the political establishment is the need to gain acceptance for a return to a more *laissez-faire* model of capitalism in which the role of state intervention is extremely limited – in contrast to the highly interventionist Keynesian model prevalent during the boom period of 1950–73 – while at the same time accommodating the private corporate sector's chronic (and growing) need for large state subsidies. Such a contradiction is becoming all the more difficult to justify while, in order to try and address the chronic fiscal crisis and mounting public debt burdens in all the industrial market economies, social welfare budgets have continued to be squeezed in the face of persistent high unemployment (see Chapter 4).

The ultimate failure of these attempts to stabilize the global market economy is, as has been suggested, perfectly consistent with experience of earlier crises that have affected the capitalist profits system over the past two hundred years. If this were not serious enough, however, at least two new long-term constraints have appeared in the last twenty years, either of which might by itself seem to undermine any lingering faith in the system's durability.

Information technology – a new threat to the power of capital

While many commentators have tried to present the information technology revolution as an opportunity to develop new industries which will form the basis of a revived economic boom, it has become increasingly apparent that it will exacerbate rather than reduce the surpluses of labour and capital which are the most serious symptoms of the crisis. This is mainly because most of the new 'industries' it has spawned, such as 'e-commerce' (selling of goods and services via the Internet), are simply substitutes for existing activities such as conventional retailing or mail order trading, and thus do not create a net increase in overall consumer demand or employment. Even more devastatingly, their effect on the demand for capital is actually proving to be negative in that they require very little investment in fixed capital (machinery and equipment) – as opposed to expenditure on software and a quite limited amount of highly skilled manpower.

This shift in the structure of the economy towards activities which are more 'knowledge-intensive' rather than capital- or labour-intensive does indeed have revolutionary implications for the capitalist system – whose original *raison d'être* was to mobilize the large amounts of capital needed to facilitate the first industrial revolution. For if the demand for capital is going into long-term decline as a result of the electronic revolution it is bound to prove even harder to justify maintaining an economic system based on the principle of maximizing profits, since there will be ever diminishing outlets for re-investment of these profits, at least in assets with a predictable or durable value. Indeed it is already widely recognized, in the frenetic speculative climate prevailing at the dawn of the new century, that accountants and investors are finding it more and more difficult to put a definitive value on companies whose assets consist increasingly of 'intangibles' of uncertain worth.[9]

Such developments put in starker relief than ever the age-old problem of the capitalist profits system: how to sustain the rate of profit on the ever-growing mass of capital when the capacity of market demand to expand continuously at a fast enough rate, so as to provide the necessary investment outlets, is inevitably finite. Given the evidence that economic growth is unlikely over the long run to be sustainable much above its historic annual average of 2 to 2.5 per cent, and that technological change will ensure that demand for fixed capital investment will actually decline below its historic average, the search for new investment opportunities will surely become more desperate than ever.[10]

Environmental constraints to growth
Just as advances in technology are now tending to undermine the role of capital in the modern economy, an unforeseen threat has arisen to the possibility of sustaining growth rates even at the historic levels that now appear increasingly inadequate to assure the sustainability of the profits system. This is the mounting evidence that unrestrained economic growth may have begun to inflict serious damage to the planetary biosphere, such that it may become counterproductive to human welfare, not to mention that of other species.

The most serious manifestation of this danger is the evidence that increased levels of economic activity may be causing global warming and thus quite abrupt changes in climate with seriously negative consequences, for example, for agriculture or the viability of habitation in certain areas. Yet at the same time different types of production and consumption are contributing to unhealthy levels of pollution of air, land and water, often because the sheer volume of pollutants has become too great to be absorbed. This is in many cases simply a function of the growth of the world's population, which has risen threefold since 1950 – a rate of expansion without historic precedent.

The implication of such developments is that steps must be taken to ensure that:

- *either* the growth in the level of global economic activity slows down to a level consistent with environmental sustainability;
- *and/or* industrial technology and patterns of development are adjusted so as to be more 'environmentally friendly'.

It should be obvious that any acceptance of the idea that policy should be geared to restricting or discouraging high rates of growth would be inimical to the survival of the profits system. In fact it is remarkable how many leading advocates of production based on lower levels of growth or more resource-efficient technology fail to recognize that their recipes would be fatal to the interests of corporations long geared to maximizing investment and consumption.[11] Yet even if ways could be found to pursue maximum growth without harming the environment, this would clearly require tighter regulation of the use of industrial and other technologies to an extent that would be incompatible with the kind of deregulated economy that western industrialized countries have been trying to create since the 1970s.

This brief account of the long-term trends in the development of the capitalist economy since the Industrial Revolution thus point to an inescapable conclusion of momentous significance. This is that, by the mid-1970s, attempts to make the demands of an economic system that is geared to maximizing the profits of unregulated private enterprise compatible with the minimum needs of the population for security and stability had definitively failed. This being the case, the obvious (but always unspoken) conclusion has been that the only way forward was:

- either to subject private enterprises to sufficient public accountability to ensure they meet the community's minimum requirements;
- or to reconcile the public to the belief that the fluctuating and uncertain levels of security which the profits system can offer are the best they can reasonably expect.

In the more pluralist modern democracies of today's industrialized world one might have supposed that the first of these options would prevail. Nevertheless, since it would clearly have entailed a massive redistribution of wealth and income – arguably amounting to the creation of a full-blown socialist economy – this has been an obviously unacceptable option for the global establishment. Given the continuing power of the latter to manipulate the political system, it has been able to evade the issue ever since the 1970s, hoping all the while that either the public would be persuaded to lower its expectations or that some miracle – such as the 'new economy' paradigm – would get it off the hook. For the US, however, the intensifying pressures of the economic crisis have further complicated the task of maintaining its global hegemony in the post-Cold War world.

IMPLICATIONS OF THE CRISIS
FOR US WORLD DOMINANCE

It is generally accepted that the drive to imperial power must be largely motivated, or at least ultimately sustained, by economic interests. The necessity of this rationale arises because, whatever the initial political justification for imposing alien rule on another country, it must offer at least a reasonable prospect of yielding some tangible economic gain to the imperial power – if only to compensate for the costs of assuring administrative control. This means that the maintenance of such power in the modern world requires the ability not only to neutralize any forces making for political or other sources of instability in the subject territories but also to assure a continuing demonstrable flow of economic benefits to the hegemonic power. Traditionally, as in the case of the British and Dutch empires, this meant that imperial policy was more or less closely geared to the national commercial or industrial interest groups which dominated the political process in those countries – in an era when only those possessing significant wealth had voting rights. In today's world, imperial policy has had to be conducted in the context of a domestic political system which is, at least in name, far more democratically accountable.

Thus the US, propelled by circumstances to a position of de facto imperial hegemony since 1945, has been forced to try and make this role consistent with the pursuit of 'United States interests' in the eyes of a domestic political constituency significantly more pluralist than the narrow commercial class that provided the political impetus to British imperial expansion in the eighteenth and nineteenth centuries. Put crudely, this has entailed ensuring that the benefits of maintaining global hegemony were not perceived by the US public to be exceeded by the costs. This in turn has meant convincing a critical mass of American opinion not only that the financial costs were not excessive but that the military burden was bearable (in terms of the level of casualties) and that the assertion of US authority over other countries was consistent with politically acceptable goals.

It nevertheless remains as true as it was in Victorian Britain that economic considerations are the decisive factor in the overall equation. Likewise the need for the capitalist economy to find new markets and investment outlets to meet its inescapable urge to expand has been just as compelling in the late twentieth century as it was perceived to be in the heyday of empire.[12] It should be noted, moreover, that there has been a strong identity of interest in this respect between the corporate sector in the US and those in other leading capitalist nations, such as Britain and France. For the latter retain significant economic interests in the Third World – not only in their former colonies – and have thus been quite readily co-opted to play their part in sustaining the *pax Americana*.

As noted above, the period of the post-war boom up to the early 1970s was broadly conducive to the international expansion of US global economic power, and of its corporate interests in particular. Since the watershed of the 1974–75 recession, however, conditions have inevitably become less favourable to expanding market and investment opportunities for US business around the world.

Moreover, while the impact of this prolonged downturn has been serious enough for the developed market economies which account for the vast bulk of world output, it has been even more severe on the countries of the Third World and, particularly since around 1990, those of the former Soviet bloc.[13] Not only have their growth rates on average declined more sharply than those of the industrial market economies; because this decline has been from a far lower base in terms of average income per head, and because income disparities in developing societies are generally far greater than in industrialized countries, it has inevitably led to much greater social devastation than has yet occurred in the richer countries (see Chapter 5).

Notwithstanding this catastrophic decline in the condition of most of the world's poor economies, the industrialized countries, led by the US, have stubbornly sought to impose on them the same model of extreme orthodoxy and liberalization that they now claim to be applying to their own much stronger economies. Such an approach – variously known as 'structural adjustment' or 'shock therapy' – has been the basis of the development strategy pursued by international aid agencies towards the Third World, and latterly ex-Communist, countries since around 1980. What makes this unbending stance so remarkable is that it has been uniformly ineffective in reviving the economic fortunes of the countries concerned – or indeed in preventing them from deteriorating still further. This truth is now obvious despite a powerful propaganda campaign, led by the IMF and World Bank, insisting that only those countries following this neo-liberal model (based on removal of controls on prices, capital movements and trade) can achieve sustainable prosperity.

The remarkable unanimity of the western donor community in support of this 'Washington consensus' has failed to disguise the fact that its advocates could not cite any instances of its succeeding. This glaring deficiency in their argument has only been underlined by attempts to claim the East Asian 'tiger' economies such as South Korea and Taiwan as examples, even though it has always been well known to serious analysts that the latter's (relative) success was largely thanks to their systematic distortion of market forces and de facto rejection of the principles of free trade.[14] Moreover, any pretence that liberalization was beneficial to the advancement of developing economies was finally exploded by the financial crisis that struck East Asia in 1997, the proximate cause of which is now recognized to have been the excessively free flows of 'hot' money in and out of the region which the ending of capital controls had made possible.

The predictable failure of these US-imposed strategies to alleviate the intensifying economic and social problems in the developing world is inevitably putting severe strain on the global political order and on the ability of the US to maintain its neo-imperialist hegemony. Thus, whereas previously it had been relatively easy for it to assure a degree of political stability in Third World states under compliant governments, since the 1970s mounting popular disaffection in the face of economic breakdown and spreading destitution and hopelessness has been more and more readily translated into civil unrest and political upheaval. In such circumstances any Third World government has to be subjected to greater pressure than ever to act in accordance with US wishes, whether or not it has been put in power as a result of a coup or other machinations inspired by Washington. Inevitably, moreover, the problem is magnified by the widespread culture of corruption and anti-democratic repression in these countries, which was effectively fostered by the US and its allies during the Cold War. Thus in these fragile states the administrations are more than ever prone to plunder the maximum from their people in as short a time as possible, mindful as they are of the continual danger of violent overthrow by one group or other of their deprived (or simply envious) fellow citizens. Against such a background, calls for improved standards of Third World governance by the US and other western countries – themselves increasingly exposed as flawed democracies[15] – appear as hypocritical as they are patronizing.

NECESSITY OF THE FREE-MARKET MYTH

Faced with the growing evidence that its strategy for reversing the economic decay of the Third World and the countries of the former Soviet bloc has manifestly failed, the response of successive US administrations has been remarkably inflexible. This seems all the more surprising in that they can hardly have been unaware of the spreading epidemic of collapsing civil order and, in more and more countries, of outright war, or that this phenomenon is significantly linked to economic breakdown in most cases. It is true that, following the disastrous setback to prospects for Third World development represented by the Mexican and East Asian financial crises of 1994 and 1997 respectively, the World Bank has been encouraged to give greater emphasis to the 'war on poverty'. However, it remains doubtful whether this is more than a largely empty public relations catchphrase, given that to date there is no sign of any willingness on the part of the US government – which effectively dictates the agenda of the World Bank and the IMF – to permit any significant deviation from its ruinous neo-liberal agenda.

It is clearly essential to consider why, in the face of such palpable failure – which is reflected in the halving (on average) of the economies of the former Soviet Union since the fall of Communism – the United States persists in trying to impose the same unworkable policies on poor countries, especially when it has to live with the highly unpalatable consequences, such as:

- a further upsurge in the already huge numbers of refugees and economic migrants fleeing impoverished Third World and ex-communist countries;
- still more outbreaks of war, either within or between states, in the regions affected by civil and political breakdown;
- growing popular disgust within the US itself and other developed countries at the destructive impact of 'structural adjustment' and what is seen by many as the malign influence of big business over official policy – as manifested in the mass demonstrations against the World Trade Organization in Seattle in late 1999 and sub-sequently at similar world gatherings in Washington, Prague and Genoa.

In truth it is hard to make sense of such a seemingly irrational strategy except in terms of some speculative conspiracy theory, particularly in the absence of any willingness among mainstream politicians or commentators to question its basic logic. Thus it is quite common, in the author's experience, to hear anecdotal support for the view that the US government is influenced by forces which regard political chaos and international or ethnic conflict as serving their political purposes, perhaps providing cover for a revival of quasi-fascist, authoritarian regimes in the western world – not to mention a boost to the armaments industry. Others have speculated that the obdurate insistence of the US on keeping the 'shock therapy' squeeze on the former Soviet bloc is driven by a desire to ensure the con-tinued weakness of its former Cold War adversary.

Yet while it is not possible, nor necessarily wise, to dismiss such notions out of hand, a somewhat more logical, if scarcely less dis-turbing, explanation for such rigidity seems far more plausible. This is the perception that, however counter-productive the structural adjustment approach, based on extreme neo-liberalism, might be, any official recognition that it contains significant flaws would open the floodgates to far-reaching state intervention in the economies not only of the developing world but of the developed world as well. Moreover, even the slightest moves in this direction would seem certain to provoke the collapse in values of financial securities which has long been threatening to occur even without such an additional danger to profitability. Hence any concession to demands for tighter control of markets or the actions of big business might rapidly turn the demise of free market capitalism into a self-fulfilling prophecy.[16]

Likewise it would clearly be fatal for the ruling élite even to admit the possibility that the survival and growth of private enterprise might owe anything to 'corporate welfare', or other forms of state protection, rather than to their own management skills or entrepreneurship. For it would not only invite demands for the private sector to be made more publicly accountable in return for the support and privileges it receives from the state; it would also call into question the élite's disproportionately greater financial rewards, which they typically justify either as the response of competitive forces to the scarcity of entrepreneurial talent or the just reward for those who are supposedly willing to risk their fortunes in the uncertain but publicly beneficial pursuit of corporate growth.[17]

Any such damage to the financial strength or autonomy of the corporate sector and its leaders would in turn be bound to weaken its immense political power, now reflected in its ability to buy the subservience of almost any political party both in the US and elsewhere. Thus it is probably quite rational for this dominant interest group to conclude that by giving an inch they would risk rapidly losing their grip on power entirely. Such a stance would, moreover, be no more than a logical extension of the position which, as suggested above, was behind their refusal to accept a greater degree of collectivism in the 1970s. Indeed, bearing in mind the huge damage, both economically and socially, that has been inflicted on so many countries, it seems difficult to explain such dysfunctional conduct of affairs except in terms of extreme desperation on the part of the ruling élite to cling to power.

SELF-CONTRADICTORY STRATEGIES

It is nevertheless paradoxical that such destructive policies are being forced on the developing world just at the moment when it has come to be seen as a more important component of the global capitalist economy. This has come about because, in their desperate search for credible investment opportunities outside the increasingly saturated markets of the industrialized countries, leading financial institutions have felt compelled to promote the emerging markets of the Third World and the ex-Soviet bloc as promising new outlets for the huge volumes of surplus capital being generated by western corporations. That this could have happened at a time when the same dominant interest groups are imposing ruinous structural adjustment programmes on these very countries might suggest a serious failure on the part of the former to coordinate their actions. It would certainly tend to refute any notion of a tight-knit conspiracy of manipulation.

In fact, given the overwhelming force of the official propaganda barrage in favour of the Washington consensus – backed by incessant Wall Street and media hype – it is hardly surprising that many investors have been induced to believe in its efficacy, especially as few of them have first-hand knowledge of the economies concerned. It should be added, moreover, that an increasing number of investor institutions have become largely reckless of prudential standards, and indeed are often motivated by a desire to seek out the riskiest opportunities – in the ever more desperate hope that they will yield the highest returns. This further paradox results from the distorted incentives offered to fund managers to take excessive risks with (other people's) money in the expectation that in the event of large-scale failure the state will bail them out in its capacity as 'lender of last resort' – a view that proved all too justified in the wake of the Mexican collapse of 1994–95.[18] Even more disturbingly, this climate of laxity has encouraged the infiltration of financial markets and institutions by criminal elements only too willing to profit from opportunities for fraud at the public's expense, as most notably in the case of the Russian banking sector in the 1990s.[19]

The appearance of such symptoms of worldwide malaise and the manifest inability of the US and the ruling global élite to resolve the unbearably conflicting pressures which they reveal point to a convergence of two crises: one of *imperialist political control*, the other of the *capitalist economic system*. Assuming, as seems virtually certain, that the relative stagnation of the global economy continues, a major financial collapse (perhaps even more catastrophic than that of 1929–33) is unavoidable. In the effort to avert such an outcome there will naturally be intensifying strains on the global political control structure. Indeed examples of this have already started to proliferate, with spreading political unrest manifesting itself in many Third World countries since the mid-1990s, including some which had but recently acquired a veneer of greater democratic legitimacy (such as Mexico, Ecuador, Côte d'Ivoire and Indonesia) after decades of corrupt authoritarian rule.

These tensions demonstrate the vulnerability of the US, just as much as any imperial power of the past, to the breakdown of the essential imperialist equation referred to earlier. For at the same time as the benefits to the US economy (or rather to the giant transnational corporations and finance houses which control the national political agenda) are dwindling in the wake of Third World collapse, the costs of maintaining control are seen to be rising – as much in terms of the country's blood and moral reputation as of its taxpayers' money. This tendency is most manifest in the evidently recurring desire of successive US administrations to disengage from Africa – a region perceived to be of little obvious national economic interest – especially since the disastrous intervention in Somalia in the early 1990s. By 2000 this had reached the point where the Clinton administration's only response to the chaos spreading across that continent was to plead with the former colonial powers to deploy troops to stem the tide (such as Britain in relation to Sierra Leone) – or else give half-hearted support to United Nations 'peacekeeping' forces, on condition that no US troops were involved.

As already noted, the feature of this contemporary order which is the most obvious source of present global tensions is the impossibility of reconciling the idea of imperialism with that of democracy. As we have also observed, the twentieth century has been the first in which, with the advent of universal suffrage, this contradiction has been a constraint to the exercise of hegemonic power by one nation state over others. Yet it is clear from the analysis in this chapter that the effort to resolve it has been focused on trying to turn the clock back rather than forward. Thus instead of accepting the need to bow to public opinion expressed through a genuine democratic process the forces of finance and commerce are seeking to resume the exclusive control of the political system that they exercised in the classic age of empire in the eighteenth and nineteenth centuries. This means not only the more or less openly corrupt suborning of officials of the supposedly sovereign governments of developing countries, but also the blatant buying of the electoral process in the developed world – such that a country like Britain now sees its allegedly democratic constitution as debauched as in the days of the 'rotten boroughs' before the Reform Act of 1832, when seats in the House of Commons were openly bought and sold and many members of parliament never found it necessary to visit their constituencies either before or after their election.

The obvious implication is not only that imperialism cannot co-exist with any meaningful form of democracy, but that capitalism suffers from the same defect. At the same time it must be presumed that the United States, whether it manages to free its body politic from the present corporate tyranny or not, will lose the will to imperial power once the economic costs of trying to maintain it are seen to exceed the gains – just as Britain and other imperial powers made the same implicit calculation in the past. It thus seems certain that the world is due for a period of prolonged upheaval and change as we enter the new century. In fashioning new structures more responsive to the increasingly complex demands of a plural global community it will be necessary to revisit most of the fundamental principles and assumptions of the present order.

CHAPTER 3

CORPORATE INTERESTS
VERSUS THE PUBLIC INTEREST

A central assumption of the ideology which underpins the present global order is that the interests of economic welfare are best served by privately owned corporations – driven by the goal of profit maximization – competing with each other for customers in a free market. This classical precept, most particularly associated with the ideas of the eighteenth-century economist Adam Smith, rests on the presumption that:

- the competitive process benefits consumers by stimulating enterprises to drive prices down and quality up in pursuit of increased business and profit;
- the profits generated can be reinvested as part of a dynamic process – mediated through a capitalistic financial system – of more or less perpetually expanding output, income and wealth.

This benign view of an economic system dominated by the private corporate sector has been most graphically captured in the famous claim of a former captain of US industry that 'what's good for General Motors is good for the United States'.[1] Yet the history of the world since the Industrial Revolution some 200 years ago provides plentiful evidence that such a crude equation is as simplistic as it is self-serving. Indeed it suggests that unrestrained competition by enterprises in pursuit of profit maximization is all too often fatal to the public interest, particularly where those enterprises are not only free of any accountability to anyone but their own shareholders but are often afforded special privileges and protection by the state. Despite this the power of corporate propaganda, ingrained in the ideology of most or all western political parties, has ensured that popular opinion remains largely unconscious of the grave deficiencies of this economic model.

THE PROBLEM WITH COMPETITION

It is perhaps not surprising that the commonsense notion that competition is generally in the public interest has retained strong popular appeal over the generations. Most people have experienced both the advantages of being able to choose between suppliers of goods or services who are genuinely competing with each other in an undistorted market and, conversely, the disadvantages of being at the mercy of a monopoly supplier or cartel which is allowed to abuse its market power at the expense of users without adequate public scrutiny or regulation. Yet, as even Adam Smith himself recognized, the theoretical benefits of competition are not easy to secure in practice, given that businessmen whose primary motivation is to maximize their profits are naturally prone to try and eliminate or neutralize any factors, such as competition, which tend to reduce them. There is thus an inherent conflict between the goal of competitive markets and that of profit maximization, with economic actors of all kinds (including trade unions as well as corporations) tending to favour competition for all other groups but their own.

Furthermore, repeated experience over the years has shown that, while competition may, under certain circumstances and for relatively short periods, provide consumers with an optimum combination of choice and value, it also has severely negative consequences which are often more lasting, particularly when combined with the pursuit of profit maximization. These inherent flaws may be considered under four main heads.

Market uncertainty

By its very nature free market competition tends to generate uncertainty and instability, particularly where the actual or potential number of competing suppliers of a given product or service is large.

The obvious reason for this is that, even if existing producers know with reasonable certainty the total size of the market demand they are seeking to meet, they cannot necessarily predict with any accuracy what the total volume of supply will be, at least beyond the very short term. Equally it is hard for producers under such conditions of 'atomistic' competition to anticipate whether or to what extent their competitors may apply cost-reducing new technology and/or improvements in quality or design such that sales of their own products may suffer a decline. Faced with such imponderables, each enterprise supplying the market tends to take whatever steps it can to overcome or minimize competition, just as classical economic theory requires that it should. Unfortunately such a response almost inevitably results, over time, in an expansion of total productive capacity well beyond the level that can be absorbed by market demand (a tendency which is reinforced by the well-known capitalist compulsion to reinvest surplus profits). Hence the competitive process is almost perfectly designed to promote

- a high degree of insecurity and instability in markets, often resulting in sharp cyclical fluctuations in output, employment and prices;
- a concentration of ownership in a diminishing number of enterprises as weaker competitors are forced out of business.

While the theory suggests that this process of attrition tends to result in the survival of only those best able to provide consumers with products giving the optimum combination of quality and price, in practice victory all too often goes to those with the deepest pockets, who are best placed to withstand a competitive price squeeze. Moreover, such financial power can also be, and frequently is, exercised to prevent new competitors entering the market, whether by means of predatory pricing to prevent new entrants from gaining market share, pressurizing distributors not to handle competitors' products or simply by buying them out through acquisition of their shares. There is thus an in-built tendency in any given product market for competition to be reduced in the long run as corporations seek to protect their investors' return on capital, to the disadvantage of the very consumers who were supposed to be the main beneficiaries of the process.

The seeming inevitability of such negative effects is reflected in the cyclical (or in some cases more or less permanent) world-wide overcapacity in major sectors of industry – including motor vehicles, steel, petrochemicals and cement. Equally, both political and financial pressures – combined with the complexity of distorting subsidies – are such that it is seldom possible to facilitate a shake-out of capacity that brings the market to any kind of equilibrium for very long. Instead the response of the major corporations involved, often with the tacit connivance of the authorities, is to operate de facto cartels or informal price-fixing arrangements so as to limit the potential disruption from competition. Well-known instances of this are the long-standing cement cartel in Britain and the effective fixing of car prices in the European Union (reflected in large and inexplicable variations in prices for identical products in different member states of the 'single market').

The need for the community to try and resist such market-distorting pressures has long been recognized in the industrial market economies by the creation of anti-monopoly legislation and institutions designed to protect the interest of consumers. However, it is also noticeable that such regulatory authorities are often susceptible to pressure to moderate their zeal in promoting competition, especially where politically influential mega-corporations can exert pressure to have the normal rules suspended to their benefit. A notorious recent case in point has been that of Microsoft Corporation, the world's dominant supplier of computer software. For, despite having an obviously monopolistic position in the global market and a consequent ability to extract super-profits from its business, the company has been able to mobilize strong political and media support for the view that this monopoly does not operate against the public interest. Consequently, it appears (at the time of writing) to have a good chance of overturning a judicial decision to make it divest parts of its business – or at least of avoiding complying with it for many years.

Imperfect access to information

Although advocates of *laissez-faire* claim as one of its central merits that it offers freedom of choice and that 'the customer is king', both theory and practice suggest this is inevitably far from being the reality. For in competitive markets profit-maximizing businesses have an obvious incentive to offer their customers products or services that are the cheapest to supply at the highest price they can get away with, other things being equal. While a rational entrepreneur will nevertheless seek, under normal circumstances, to offer customers optimum value for money in terms of quality and price (in order to establish and retain their loyalty) it is natural for them to seek to cut corners and restrict the consumer's freedom of choice where share-holder pressures to maintain or increase profitability demand it. Under such conditions the customer all too easily becomes an unsuspecting victim, particularly in the absence of ready access to adequate information regarding the quality of products and the alternative choices that may be available.

Consumer protection regulations (at least in industrialized countries) are designed to overcome this constraint and to compensate for the fact that consumers often find it costly and unrewarding to switch suppliers in markets where competition may anyway be restricted. However, experience has shown that, where pressures to maintain profits are intensifying and governments are susceptible to the influence of strong corporate lobbies, controls are liable to be relaxed at the expense of consumers. The dangers of such market failure have been particularly evident in the phase of deregulation which most developed economies have been undergoing since the early 1980s. Most conspicuously in Britain it seems likely that the relaxation of controls and standards in the area of animal husbandry and meat processing contributed to the major outbreaks of BSE, foot-and-mouth disease and E-coli poisoning during this period, which have imposed such immense cost not only on consumers but on the economy as a whole.

Wasteful duplication of capacity

Aside from the tendency of uncontrolled competition to result in cyclical over-investment in most markets, there are also many in-

stances where the very nature of a market makes it inherently difficult
and/or very expensive to ensure that the public can benefit from
genuine competition. This applies in particular to those sectors of
the economy requiring substantial investment in infrastructure networks – such as trunk roads, railways, water supply, energy distribution and telecommunications. For in such cases the creation of
competing networks has generally been shown to be uneconomic
because of the need to undertake double or treble the amount of
capital expenditure to provide a service which can quite easily be
supplied from a single network – a consideration which until the
1980s was reflected in the general acceptance that such public services were 'natural monopolies'.[2] Likewise in the case of industries,
such as manufacture of defence equipment, serving a very limited
market (often comprising only their own national government) but
requiring massive investment in research and development as well as
fixed capital, it is clearly highly inefficient to require competitive
bids, as noted even by a right-wing former defence secretary in
Britain.[3]

    This problem has been highlighted as a result of the privatization
of utilities and other natural monopolies in Britain and elsewhere in
the 1980s and 1990s, where it has been necessary to subject key areas
of management (particularly pricing) to supervision by a public regulator – notwithstanding half-hearted attempts to introduce competition. It is thus ironic that a policy which was ostensibly intended to
reinvigorate the previously state-owned monopolies by subjecting
them to the pressures of the competitive market-place has only served
to emphasize the difficulty of securing competition in a way that
genuinely benefits consumers.

    It should be noted in addition that the merits of genuinely free
competition – viewed as a Darwinian struggle for survival – have
been little appreciated outside the industrialized west. For traditionally
in Japan and other East Asian countries, and even in European
countries such as France, there has been scant belief in the merits of
'creative destruction', as preached by Schumpeter and other members
of the pre-war Austrian school of *laissez-faire* economists. Nowadays,
indeed, there are probably few outside the ranks of academic theore-
ticians of the far Right who would claim to believe that investment

in building new factories only for them to be closed down once total capacity is found to be surplus to requirements can be equated with economic efficiency. This may well explain why, in Japan, Korea, Thailand and elsewhere in East Asia, it has proved particularly hard to enforce the 'restructuring', let alone the liquidation, of so many technically bankrupt companies in the wake of the economic downturn they have experienced since the start of the 1990s.

Financial destabilization

As already noted, the combination of competitive markets and the compulsion to maximize profits provides a powerful impetus to over-investment under the normal capitalist dynamic. This tendency, stemming from what has long been recognized as the chronic inability of demand growth to keep pace with supply,[4] is at the root of the traditional capitalist 'business cycle' of boom and bust, resulting in recurrent bouts of recession and unemployment, often with devastating social consequences.[5] A particularly damaging aspect of this downward phase of the cycle is the typically high level of bad debts affecting the financial system, often leading – as in the United States in the slump of 1929–31 – to mass failure of banks and prolonged paralysis of their lending capacity.

Notwithstanding these rather serious weaknesses the defenders of the competitive market model continue to stress its unique dynamism in providing the impetus for technological innovation, which they argue could not have occurred at the speed it has since the Industrial Revolution without the spur of capitalist competition. Yet while it is certainly true that enterprises that are driven by the profit motive tend to be quicker to exploit technological innovation than ones that are not where there is a perceived opportunity to make a large return on the capital invested, the converse is also true. For technological change, which is very often the result of state-financed research programmes, may often occur in a way that threatens to undermine the profitability of capital investment based on existing technology. Hence it is sometimes found that manufacturing companies with an established position in a market are slow to introduce improved technology and likewise seek to obstruct its introduction by competitors.[6]

THE INEVITABILITY OF STATE INTERVENTION

Progressively, over the first two hundred years or so following the Industrial Revolution, it came to be recognized that the disastrous social and economic consequences of more or less unrestrained competition and pursuit of profit were ultimately not tolerable. For, however 'efficient' the competitive model might be in minimizing 'short-run marginal costs', in the longer term it was bound to produce results that could only be regarded as seriously inefficient from the perspective of the community as a whole. Above all, the catastrophe of the 1930s – when mass unemployment and widespread financial ruin were clearly central causes of the spread of Fascism and the slide into the unprecedented destruction of World War II – was seen by 1945 as a lesson that could not be ignored. Thus even leaders of the political Right were moved to accept that *laissez-faire* was 'as dead as the slave trade'.[7]

In fact a significant degree of state intervention in the economy had always been accepted – and indeed demanded – in Europe, both before and after the Industrial Revolution, although this was for the most part directed at protecting the interests of the wealthy and the entrepreneurial class at a time when the masses had still not been enfranchised. This involved, for example, not only the enactment and enforcement of laws severely restricting the rights of workers to bargain for humane terms of employment, but also extending a privileged limitation of legal liability to all shareholding companies. What was different after 1945 was that for the first time the purpose of such intervention was seen as being to avert the worst social consequences of cyclical fluctuations of the economy and to promote 'full employment', as proclaimed in numerous policy documents of the period.[8]

Hence by 1945 it was universally recognized that the damaging side-effects of the traditional competitive model of capitalism were such as to render it incompatible with the needs of a modern society without the application of offsetting state intervention.[9] Indeed it has been implicitly accepted ever since that such intervention – including extensive public subsidy of private businesses – is essential to economic stability despite the distortion of market forces that results. Moreover, as already noted, this has been just as true of the period since the late 1970s when neo-liberal ideology has been in the ascendant, even though the main focus of state intervention has been more on corporate than on social welfare.

INTENSIFYING CONTRADICTIONS

It is hard to see how the ruling global establishment can much longer avoid responding to compelling questions about the continued justification for state subsidization and protection of private enterprise amid intensifying worldwide social misery and 'public squalor'. For, as already noted, it is by now de facto accepted by all – notwithstanding the rhetoric – that an economic model based on unrestrained competition is unworkable from just about any point of view. Yet if instead the state is to permit – and indeed underwrite – a watered-down competitive model dominated by enterprises which are accountable exclusively to their private owners, this is almost bound to produce unacceptable conflicts between private and public interests. Under a meaningful democracy such conflicts must normally be resolved in favour of the perceived public interest. Hence, for example, where it is deemed appropriate to provide a public subsidy of private profit in order to keep an enterprise in business it must also require the beneficiary company to adhere to specific commitments as a condition of support – whether in terms of investment, employment or price levels. In the final analysis, privately owned businesses benefiting from publicly guaranteed privilege or protection (e.g. limited liability) should be allowed to operate only to the extent that they accept a necessary degree of public accountability. In short, there will need to be some guarantee that what is good for General Motors (or Microsoft) does indeed bring benefits to the rest of the community.

It is worth recalling that in the pre-industrial era such logic was implicitly accepted in the relatively rare cases where companies were granted more or less exclusive licences to trade in certain areas or exploit particular resources. Thus, for example, it was always understood that the chartered East India companies of England, France and the Netherlands, founded in the seventeenth century, were accountable and ultimately subservient to the state. Indeed the implicit notion behind this type of organization – of protection being provided in return for acceptance of obligation – was essentially a feudal one. As such it was of course anathema to Adam Smith and other prophets of bourgeois liberalism. On the other hand, it is clearly implicit in the Keynesian model that state intervention in support of private sector corporations was expected to ensure that the latter helped to deliver key social objectives such as full employment. But what has clearly been lacking in most western countries is any explicit or legally binding guarantee that obliges companies to fulfil certain commitments on pain of either loss of tax and other privileges, or ultimately state expropriation of their assets. Ironically the nearest approach among contemporary market economies to a model requiring a specific *quid pro quo* from corporate beneficiaries of state support is to be found in East Asian states such as Japan and Korea – although there is still no formal obligation involved and the corporate relationship with government in these countries has tended to degenerate into one of corruption and cronyism.[10]

In fact events since the failure of Keynesian corporatism became manifest in the 1970s have served to demonstrate the underlying realities of political power and accountability in the industrial market economies. For so far from private corporations being held to account for their inability to deliver the growth and employment which the public might have expected of them, rather the reverse has happened. Thus from the late 1970s it became the conventional political wisdom that employees and social welfare claimants (the mass of the population) must be pilloried for their excessive demands on the national income at the expense of corporate profits, the low level of which was held to be a major cause of the decline in growth of output and employment. The British Labour government of 1974–79 even went so far as to institute a 'social contract' with the trade union leadership, according to which a return to full employment could only be delivered on condition that organized labour would severely limit its demands for increased wages or improvements in welfare benefits. Furthermore, even when by the 1980s most western governments had abandoned the pretence that full employment was still on the agenda – while many had also weakened their commitment to maintain adequate levels of social welfare – there was no question of any cuts in corporate welfare. On the contrary, as already noted, tax breaks and subsidies for the private corporate sector became more abundant than ever, even as the increasingly pro-business media and political establishment derided corporatism and lauded the benefits of 'rolling back the frontiers of the state'.

A striking example of this hypocrisy in action has been the vogue in the 1980s and 1990s for using large amounts of public money to promote 'urban regeneration' in the numerous cities in the industrialized west that have suffered serious rundown as a result of economic stagnation and consequent industrial decline. This trend, which originated in certain US cities in the 1970s but became politically fashionable all over North America and western Europe, involved the expenditure of tens of billions of dollars of taxpayers' money (overall) on prestige construction projects and improved urban infrastructure. The ostensible purpose of these schemes has been to stimulate an inflow of substantially greater amounts of private investment into the affected areas – attracted by the enhanced urban environment – in job-creating new enterprises. In practice, however, the main effect has been to create short-term opportunities for profitable real estate speculation, but with little or no lasting benefit to the community in terms of new jobs or improvement to the quality of those lives blighted by industrial decline.[11]

Perhaps the most blatant of all expressions of this double standard is the safety net provided to the financial sector by governments (usually through the central bank) acting as lenders of last resort. The extent of this implicit guarantee – justified by the need to protect the public against a total collapse of the banking system such as occurred in the 1930s – is now so pervasive that it has effectively destroyed the most basic mechanisms of the so-called 'free' market. This is because, by inducing a belief among investors and bankers that they are likely to be bailed out by the state in the event of a large loan turning sour (at least if it is big enough to threaten a chain reaction of bankruptcies throughout the system), it has created a widespread climate of what is referred to as 'moral hazard'. The potential dangers of this distortion of market forces have only been intensified by the breathtaking extremes of banking deregulation in the United States, culminating in the Gramm–Leach–Bliley Act, signed by President Clinton in 1999.[12] This has created an ever more irresistible temptation for financial and non-financial enterprises alike to make risky speculative investments in the expectation that they will make a fortune if successful and will lose little more than their jobs if the gamble fails.

Moreover, it has been noticeable during the financial bubble of 1998–2001 that the US authorities, led by Alan Greenspan, Chairman of the Federal Reserve Board, have been very willing to try and extend this safety net for the banks to the financial markets as a whole by sharply cutting interest rates whenever there has appeared to be imminent danger of market meltdown. From such manipulative intervention in the market it could have seemed but a short step to public funds being deployed to buy shares in order to support the level of stock indices.[13] Indeed this already happens quite openly in Far Eastern markets such as Japan, Taiwan and Hong Kong, a practice which has evoked remarkably little criticism from supposed free market ideologues in the west.

Increasingly it has also come to be recognized that financial markets exposed to such moral hazard are bound to have a seriously distorting effect on the entire economy, especially where the media and the major political parties are beholden to the financial interests involved and thus easily persuaded to help justify and promote massive investment in assets of dubious worth. Thus it is now clear that the whole 'dot.com bubble' of 1999–2000 was possible only because investors and financial institutions were encouraged to speculate in the shares of internet companies with scarcely any sales and little tangible prospect of making profits. This in turn could happen only because investors were led to believe that credit could be endlessly expanded by a financial sector which was effectively out of official control, thanks to banking deregulation, but was nevertheless also perceived to be fully underwritten by the US authorities. Hence, as a leading Wall Street operator reflected after the bursting of the bubble, 'for the dot.coms capital was essentially free'.[14] Obviously, moreover, to the extent that such 'new economy' enterprises were being effectively subsidized by this flow of free capital, they were enabled to compete unfairly with existing businesses. As a result, for example, on-line retailers of books (such as Amazon.com) were in a position to undercut conventional high-street booksellers, who were required to make at least some return on their capital employed, thus driving many of them out of business.

FROM MORAL HAZARD TO LEGITIMIZED CRIME

The market-distorting tendencies described above can readily be seen as symptoms of the ruling élite's determination, referred to in the last chapter, never to accept either that

- market forces should be allowed to assert themselves in a way that could seriously threaten the élite's own wealth, above all by letting the growing surplus of capital be reflected in its devaluation on financial markets; nor that
- a collectivist alternative should replace the 'free-market' profits system which is the basis of the élite's political power.

We have observed how, as a result of this basic resolve, the practices of Keynesian corporatist intervention and neo-liberal deregulation have combined to create dangerous conflicts of interest, or even to subvert the entire rationale of the capitalist market system. Yet in view of the chronic failure of this approach to resolve the problems of global economic stagnation since the 1970s it is perhaps not surprising that practices have been encouraged which are not merely contrary to the public interest but amount to a negation of such fundamental constitutional principles as property rights and the rule of law.

Such tendencies were first apparent in the 1980s when, for example, there was an outbreak of fraudulent lending by the newly liberalized savings and loan institutions in the US, whose deposits nevertheless continued to be insured by the Federal government. The outcome of this scandal, in which leading political figures and even organized crime were widely rumoured to have had a hand but which did not result in any prosecutions, was a bail-out costing taxpayers some US$150 billion. More recently there has been widespread evidence, on both sides of the Atlantic, of systematic misinformation, or even false accounting, by companies and financial institutions desperate to sell securities at a price far higher than could be justified by an objective appraisal of their true underlying value.

This tendency has become so pervasive, particularly in the US, that it has prompted the Chairman of the Securities and Exchange Commission (SEC) – the Federal government watchdog charged with supervising the financial markets – to issue a series of public warnings of the potential dangers, even though the SEC appears legally powerless to prevent such practices.[15] Similar problems have been identified in Britain and have started to worry the authorities there. However, the SEC's weakness in the face of the power and influence of the financial services industry is evident, as witness its inability in January 2000 to do more than censure the US arm of Price Waterhouse (the major auditing and consultancy group) for systematic violation of its rules on auditor independence. Hence there is little prospect of combating what amount to legalized abuses without substantially reversing the process of deregulation and making the independence of both financial analysts and auditors legally enforceable, thereby reducing the incentives or opportunities for them to produce distorted reports.

It is perhaps only fair to point out that such abuses have come to be tolerated as part of a culture, regularly endorsed by official pronouncements, which regards the maintaining of 'confidence' in the financial markets as a public good. Indeed President Franklin Roosevelt's famous pronouncement in the depths of the 1930s Depression that 'the only thing we have to fear is fear itself'[16] might well serve as the motto of the corporatist era of capitalism. Yet in a period of deregulated markets and almost unbridled scope for conflicts of interest the fine line between putting a positive spin on economic and financial market developments and the peddling of clearly fraudulent misinformation has become increasingly blurred. Indeed the worry must be, as reflected in the warnings of Chairman Arthur Levitt of the SEC, that official acceptance of such dishonest practices will ultimately increase the public perception that the capital markets are nothing but a state-sponsored pyramid scheme in which only the foolhardy or those with inside information would invest their money.

Such fears are given added credibility by the manifest collapse of investors' faith in the Japanese stock market, well known for the chronic incidence of government-inspired manipulation. This is reflected in the continuing depression of the Nikkei share index, at levels (in mid-2001) only about one-third of those from which it crashed in 1989–90. There are already ominous signs of what this might portend for the capitalist establishment as the crisis unfolds across the world. In both Germany and the United States groups of investors have already (early 2001) initiated moves to try and sue companies for providing misleading information in share prospectuses issued prior to the dramatic collapse of the stock market 'technology bubble' in 2000, in breach of capital market regulations.

Far more alarming for the authorities, however, is what the probable breakdown of the financial system, and the associated fall in the value of securities, could mean for the scores of millions of people in the developed world (especially the Anglo-Saxon countries) whose livelihoods have come to depend on ever-rising stock markets. In particular, they must be worried that large numbers of those who have been encouraged, or in many cases effectively compelled, to contribute to funded pension schemes, in the belief that this would assure them a secure income in retirement, will face virtual destitution. Indeed, in view of the potential scale of this disaster, it seems plausible to suppose that history will ultimately come to regard the state-subsidized funded pensions business of the late twentieth century as the greatest confidence trick of all time, dwarfing the South Sea Bubble or John Law's Mississippi scheme of the eighteenth century. The enormity of the crime will doubtless seem all the greater to the extent that the Bush administration succeeds in implementing its proposal to invest Social Security funds (the US state pension scheme) in stocks and shares in a last desperate attempt to avert a market crash by injecting liquidity into it.

In view of this terrifying and very real prospect, and its potentially fatal repercussions for the wealth and political power of the ruling élite, it is legitimate to suspect that governments are increasingly prepared to acquiesce in the involvement of criminal elements and methods in the process of trying to shore up the crumbling edifice. The possibility that such methods, which have long been more or less openly accepted by western governments in the conduct of their client states in the Third World, are now becoming endemic in the US itself is suggested by the increasingly insouciant attitude of its government to financial crime. Thus the incoming Bush administration in 2001 quickly announced its desire to limit severely, if not halt completely, international moves to limit the scope for concealment of illicit financial transactions. Such measures included attempts to restrict the more damaging consequences of the proliferation of off-shore tax havens (see Chapter 4) and to crack down on money laundering by and through banks.[17] Given that these efforts had been supported by the preceding Clinton administration, there are obvious grounds for suspecting that the Bush regime may have been responding to pressure from interests associated with organized crime in adopting this line – notwithstanding its attempts to justify it in terms of *laissez-faire* principles.

THE WEAKNESS OF WESTERN DEMOCRACY

We have described above the distortions and contradictions produced in the late twentieth century by a deregulated global economy dominated by profit-driven, privately owned corporations, which at the same time benefit from a commitment by the state to keep them afloat with massive protection and subsidies. We have also observed how this deadly combination has not only resulted in a seriously unbalanced and dysfunctional (not to say criminal) economic order but has even turned into a total negation of the *laissez-faire* ideology professed by its architects. That such a perverse and chaotic outcome could have been contrived by a western global leadership which not only proclaims its commitment to the ideal of democratic accountability but has access to technology and social scientific insights of unprecedented sophistication clearly calls for some explanation.

At one level it is wholly understandable that the ruling global establishment (dominated by the US) should obdurately resist any moves to loosen their tight grip on the levers of economic power, let alone to permit any reallocation of economic resources such as to favour the wider public interest at the expense of the corporate interest. For history is replete with examples, up to and including the now fallen Soviet Union, of regimes dominated by unrepresentative minorities which felt themselves unable to concede any change without risking a total undermining of their power.[18] On the other hand, such regimes in the past have invariably been authoritarian autocracies without any tradition of democratic accountability. What seems quite remarkable at the dawn of the twenty-first century is that, after two hundred years in which democratic constitutions have been established more or less throughout the western world (embodying political pluralism and freedom of expression), any meaningful dissent from the neo-liberal consensus has been so effectively stifled.

While it is difficult to offer a wholly satisfactory explanation for such extraordinary ideological conformity in face of the manifest threat of systemic failure, it seems likely to be significantly connected with:

- The enormous concentration of financial resources in the hands of a relatively small number of large private-sector corporations which are accountable to nobody but themselves.[19] This wealth is translated into political power by means of the huge and ever-expanding contributions made (quite legally) by these organizations to the financing of political parties. This phenomenon is most conspicuous in the US, where the scale of such corporate funding is estimated to have reached around US$3 billion in the federal elections of 2000, still, be it noted, a modest sum compared to the massive pay-off corporate America receives through federal spending programmes, subsidies and tax-breaks. The stranglehold

which big business has thus gained over the political process and
the agenda of mainstream parties in all industrialized countries is
of course further reinforced by its effective control of the press
and other mass media. The significance of this influence was
graphically illustrated by the remarkable and very public decision
of Tony Blair (British Prime Minister since 1997), while still leader
of the opposition, to travel ten thousand miles to Australia to seek
the support of Rupert Murdoch, the international media magnate
who controls several national newspapers in Britain, in the forth-
coming election. Such developments might seem to justify the
conclusion that western political processes are now scarcely less
susceptible to the influence of big money than they were in the
days before the Reform Act of 1832, when almost anyone with
enough wealth could simply buy themselves a seat in Parliament.
A similar reflection is prompted by the willingness of the Italian
people to elect Silvio Berlusconi as their prime minister (in 1994
and again in 2001), a man whose only qualification for the job
was that he was the wealthiest man in the country and controlled
all the private television networks.

• The collapse of the Soviet Union and its empire of satellites in
1988–91 amid the spectacular failure of the centrally planned economic system to which it was dedicated. This watershed event
naturally gave a huge propaganda boost to right-wing ideologues
and supporters of *laissez-faire* in the west, and by the same token
had the effect of marginalizing, if not totally silencing, advocates
of more collectivist economic models.

For all its refusal to accept the legitimacy of concern over the way
the public interest is being subordinated to that of the private sector,
there are some signs that the global establishment recognizes the
existence of this contradiction and the need to make some gesture
towards mitigating it. Major corporations have, of course, for many
years devoted considerable resources to enhancing their public image
in an effort to convince the world that they are benign organizations
deeply committed to advancing the general welfare of the community. Yet growing hostility to them in recent years, fuelled by a series
of public relations disasters, has made some of them aware of the

need for more concrete action. Thus in 2001, following the dramatic climbdown of the major pharmaceutical transnationals over demands that they allow the supply of anti-AIDS drugs at affordable prices in South Africa, the Swiss company Novartis decided to make available its new anti-leukaemia treatment free of charge to low-income patients in the US. The most remarkable aspect of such a gesture, however, is that it only serves to highlight the anomaly of a privileged private corporation having such unaccountable power of life and death in a modern society.

Another recently fashionable palliative designed to blunt criticisms of excessive corporate power has been the suggestion that the interests of 'stakeholders' (i.e. employees, consumers and taxpayers) could appropriately be given representation alongside those of shareholders in the management of corporations.[20] However, as demonstrated by the introduction of 'stakeholder laws' in many US states, there is no way in which such representation can be more than symbolic in the absence of an actual public sector shareholding. A similar empty formula which receives much lip-service from western governments and bodies such as the World Bank is the need to enhance the role of 'civil society' alongside corporations in influencing decisions relating to economic development. Yet to the extent that it can be determined what this expression refers to (whether charities, community associations or other informal bodies), it is clear that their most essential feature in the eyes of the establishment is that they must have no statutory representative authority and be essentially 'non-governmental', that is to say, legally powerless.

IMPENDING DISINTEGRATION

Yet in spite of all its apparent success in holding back the tide of change, the ruling élite is manifestly failing in its efforts to bring about a sustained global recovery from the chronic decline in growth rates which has occurred since the early 1970s, notwithstanding the impressive revival of US growth in the 1990s. Indeed it has become progressively more problematic since the late 1980s to maintain the illusion that good times are just around the corner, or indeed to escape the dire consequences of the ever greater market distortions and conflicts of interest that have been created in the attempt to postpone the day of reckoning. We have already observed how successive measures to deregulate, to manipulate and to underwrite the financial markets have created pressures that are by now intolerable.

A related unfolding disaster, which threatens serious damage to the corporate sector and the rest of the community alike, is the unravelling of the great privatization gamble of the post-1980 period. For as events all over the world increasingly demonstrate, attempts to turn public utilities into sustainably profitable investments for the private sector have an almost unavoidable tendency to come into conflict with the public's demand for reliable and affordable power, water, telecommunications, public transport and other essential services. The manifest impossibility of reconciling these objectives has been most devastatingly exemplified by the virtual collapse of the privatized British rail network in 2000–01, which left even some of the most hardened free market advocates clamouring for the system to be returned to public ownership.[21]

There can be little doubt that the demand for a renewal of such direct state intervention in the world's industrialized economies is set to intensify dramatically in the first decade of the new century. For not only will governments be called on to bail out or effectively expropriate privatized public utilities which either can no longer meet the demands of their shareholders or else are unable to meet the conditions of their franchises; they will also have to rescue the many funded pension schemes (of which the Equitable Life failure in Britain in 2000 is simply the forerunner) from insolvency caused by the coming prolonged downturn in the securities markets, as well as the inevitable large crop of other financial institutions that will once again fall foul of 'moral hazard'. At the same time, the inevitable credit squeeze resulting from this setback to the financial sector is bound to feed through to a sustained recession in the economy as a whole, which in turn will entail a large rise in state welfare expenditure to combat spreading unemployment and social deprivation.

As the state is once again called on to clear up the débris of an economic disaster stemming from capitalism's inherent instability, it is not possible to make even an approximate estimate of the scale of the cost to taxpayers round the world. Yet it is certain to result in a further massive rise in public indebtedness as shrinking output and falling share prices are reflected in falling state revenues, thereby pushing the United States and all other OECD countries back into the chronic fiscal deficit from which many of them thought they had escaped by the end of the 1990s. In such circumstances it will certainly prove impossible to cover this deficit by raising tax rates significantly, since this would only tend to exacerbate the recession. Even worse, it may well, at least in the short run, be almost as difficult to fill the potentially large fiscal gap by borrowing at an affordable cost, to the extent that the credit squeeze may push real interest rates higher. In desperation governments may therefore be tempted to cover part of the revenue shortfall by printing money, thus risking a sharp rise in inflation – or rather 'stagflation',[22] as it is more likely to be – and a loss of public confidence in paper currencies. As a last resort governments may simply renege on many of their key commitments, resulting in a still more serious decline in public services and perhaps the total abandonment of the welfare state.

Whatever the precise nature and extent of the damage caused by the coming global economic downturn, it can be confidently predicted that it will be severe enough to cause misery in the industrialized world on a scale worse than on any similar occasion since World War II, if not in the entire twentieth century. Moreover, given: (i) the huge overhang of excess capacity resulting from the massive over-investment encouraged by the prolonged distortion of markets; and (ii) the unprecedented level of bad debts that will need to be unwound, it can likewise be expected that any recovery will at best take many years to materialize. This prospect must in turn prompt the fear that, as in the case of the last great global depression in the 1930s, the consequent social upheavals and political disaffection will give rise to irrational and dangerous political forces akin to those of Nazism.

In such a fraught world environment it seems plausible to suppose, indeed to hope, that forces of sanity may start to emerge and demand that the world never again be subjected to the ruinous anarchy of the free market. In order to be taken seriously, however, they will need to advance, at least in outline, proposals for a more sustainable economic order. In light of the preceding analysis, there can be no doubt that the first and most essential requirement of such an alternative model must be to establish the principle that privately owned corporations will receive protection and benefits from the state only if they accept a minimum degree of accountability to the community. Of equal importance will be the need for constitutional laws which preclude the possibility of private corporations, or any other sectional interest, taking control of the democratic process in the way that all too easily happens at present. Moreover, as will be shown in the next chapters, a more viable economic order will need to be far more inclusive, both within and across national boundaries, than the capitalist profits system could ever be.

CHAPTER 4

THE WORLD TRADE SYSTEM: A STUDY IN THE FAILURE OF GLOBALIZATION

We have already shown how market distortions are bound to vitiate 'free' competition within the limited confines of a relatively small national economy. It is not surprising to find, therefore, that such distortions are an even more unavoidable factor in the context of international trade and that consequently any gains from supposedly free international trade are either largely illusory or far outweighed by the costs.

Needless to say, this conclusion is the opposite of that advanced by conventional economic theory, which still rests primarily on the 'law' of comparative advantage derived originally from the ideas advanced by the classical economist David Ricardo in the early nineteenth century.[1] According to this theory each country benefits from the free exchange of goods and services to the extent that, in so doing, it is enabled to meet its demand for them from the most cost-effective source and thus to devote its own productive factors to economic activities in which it is most competitive, thereby achieving the most efficient and profitable allocation of resources.

In the light of experience over the last two centuries and of the insights gained by economists and others over that period the durability of this simplistic theory may be considered remarkable. Arguably, it is true, it could well have seemed an adequate explanation of why countries might gain from trading with each other in Ricardo's day, when the Industrial Revolution had hardly begun to spread outside Britain and the pattern of international exchanges was far less complex than it was later to become. Yet its essential crudeness and increasing irrelevance to determining the global pattern of production and trade have since been demonstrated all too frequently. This point can be substantiated by reference to the following central realities.

CHRONIC GLOBAL SURPLUS OF CAPACITY

Most economists know it is inconceivable that the benefits of free trade posited by classical theory can apply uniformly except under conditions of more or less full employment of productive factors in all countries.[2] Yet not only have such conditions never come close to prevailing globally; they have never been further from realization than they are today.

The most obvious symptom of this problem is the chronic, and manifestly growing, incidence of global excess labour supply. Unfortunately the best-known measure of it, the statistics of registered unemployed, has largely lost what little reliability it may have had in the past. This is because of a general and understandable tendency for unemployed workers not to register unless they are entitled to claim unemployment benefit, particularly during periods of prolonged job scarcity. Hence it has always been recognized that unemployment statistics are highly unreliable in countries where such benefits are negligible or non-existent – as in virtually all Third World states, where indeed such data are generally not even compiled. Furthermore, in a number of developed (OECD) countries, particularly outside continental Europe, those out of work have been increasingly inhibited from registering since the 1970s, either by dwindling real levels of benefit entitlement or as a result of governments imposing more onerous conditions on claimants. Such measures, it should be stressed, have not just been aimed at restricting the size of the welfare bill; they are also designed to massage down the 'headline' total of unemployed, which has remained politically sensitive even after the effective abandonment of full employment as a central policy goal. To this end the authorities in Britain have taken steps to deter unemployed people from applying for benefit or else to reclassify them as beneficiaries of other welfare programmes. Such devices include placing the jobless on government retraining or subsidized

job schemes and redefining them as sick or disabled. As a result of
the latter adjustment, in many parts of Britain as much as 20 per
cent of the working population is officially classified as sick, whereas
an undistorted classification of those not working would, according
to some estimates, lead to a doubling of the official rate of unemployment (to around 12 per cent as of 1999).[3]

Still more brazen distortions have occurred in the United States,
where official figures indicate that by 2000 (thanks to the country's
vaunted 'economic miracle' of the 1990s) the unemployment ratio
had fallen to 4 per cent of the labour force, even lower than the
levels attained there during the boom years of the 1960s. However,
among other things, these data leave out of account the huge increase
in the US prison population since 1980, such that by the end of the
century 2 per cent of male adults were in jail, while another 5 per
cent were on parole or probation. Allowing for these groups, and the
rest of the substantial US 'underclass', a distinguished British economist estimated in 1997 that the true level of male unemployment
was broadly similar as between the US, Britain and continental
Europe – at 11 per cent or more.[4] Thus, even though there was
clearly some reduction of these levels during the remaining years of
the 'bubble economy' (1997–2000) it is fair to assume that the true
average ratio of unemployment in the OECD countries is still of the
order of 9 per cent – or three times that which prevailed in the
1960–73 period. This reality needs to be set against the claims of
Gordon Brown, British Chancellor of the Exchequer since 1997,
that a return to full employment is just around the corner.[5]

Yet while excess labour capacity has become a structural weakness
in the economies of the developed world since the 1970s, it has
always been one in the developing world. As noted above, meaningful statistics of unemployment have never existed for Third World
countries and ratios are impossible to estimate in such a way as to
permit a reliable comparison with the industrial market economies.
Nevertheless it is evident from the chronically low levels of formal
employment in nearly all these states and the extremely low wage
rates which continue to prevail there (averaging less than 10 per cent
of OECD levels) that their surplus labour capacity would equate to

an unemployment ratio of not less than 20–25 per cent expressed on a similar basis to that applied in OECD countries.[6] Moreover, it seems equally clear that (taking the Third World as a whole) this position continues to deteriorate, since although population growth rates in these countries have slowed markedly since the 1970s, so has the overall growth in employment opportunities.

Equally, the problem of global capacity surplus has been aggravated since the 1970s by the impact of technology in raising the productivity of both capital and labour. Moreover the impact of this phenomenon – driven mainly by innovation in the field of information technology – seems likely to continue indefinitely. Hence, given that there is little reason to expect global growth rates to average more than 2–3 per cent annually over the long term, the prospect must be that the world's already massive surplus capacity will grow rather than shrink for the foreseeable future.

In such circumstances it is hardly surprising to find that no country or local community is inclined to accept the unrequited loss of employment, income and tax revenue that may result from permitting free competition from imports. Indeed, as overcapacity has increased and competition intensified in recent decades those governments which could afford it have also felt constrained to subsidize exports in a determined effort to maintain growth and employment at home.[7] The cumulative effect of this tendency has been to promote systematic global oversupply of goods and services of all kinds, from beef to coffee and from steel to insurance, such that the true free market world price frequently falls below the cost of production of even the most efficient supplier. Yet even in the face of this obvious reality the vast majority of mainstream economists and western political leaders have, ever since World War II, continued to preach the merits of free trade with undiminished zeal.

THE DE FACTO REJECTION OF FREE TRADE

In reality there is a total lack of historical evidence that any country has ever attained the status of an advanced industrialized economy (with above average living standards) by opening its domestic market to imports without any form of protection for local producers. Indeed it is arguable that no country has ever practised anything resembling free trade, with the possible exception of Britain between 1860 and 1914,[8] although it is noteworthy that this was also the period when the British state first began significant indirect subsidization of enterprise by assuming a central role as the provider of key public services, such as water, power, telecommunications and education. It is more important, however, to note that this was the one moment when Britain, the pioneer of the Industrial Revolution, felt that it had such a competitive lead over other industrializing countries that it was in its interests to act as global champion of free trade by opening its markets. Furthermore, it arguably fitted with the powerful impulse in Britain to open up overseas markets and investment opportunities at a time when it was still unique in the huge size of the surplus capital it was generating.[9] Not surprisingly, its chief emerging competitors (Germany and the United States) declined to open their markets in return. In fact these attitudes reflect a more real and enduring feature of trade policy over the centuries. This is the idea, usually referred to as 'mercantilism', that the pattern of a country's trade is intimately linked to its economic and military strength and hence to its international power and influence, and that therefore it is far too important to be determined at the whim of supposedly uncontrolled market forces.

In relation to more recent history strenuous attempts have been made by the advocates of 'globalization' to demonstrate that the pursuit of free trade has been a key ingredient in the success of developing countries, particularly the East Asian 'tiger' economies, in moving closer to industrialized status. Undaunted by the obvious reality that these states (with the possible exception of the wholly untypical case of Hong Kong) have practised thoroughgoing protection of their export-oriented manufacturing sectors, these analysts have not scrupled to resort to a shameless perversion of economic logic to try and prove the opposite. Thus it has actually been claimed that South Korea's trade regime (combining both strong protection against imports and heavy subsidization of exports) could be defined as 'virtual free trade', on the grounds that one can be said to cancel out the effects of the other,[10] even though it should be obvious to anyone with the most elementary grasp of economics that both these types of intervention are protectionist and that their effect is therefore cumulative rather than mutually self-cancelling.

THE FANTASY OF THE 'LEVEL PLAYING FIELD'

One of the key reasons why there is virtually no willing acceptance of the principle of free trade and such widespread deviations from it in practice is that the perception can so easily arise that competition is not taking place on equal terms. This is not only because nations which are potential trading partners may treat each other's exports differently or may appear to apply differing levels of subsidy (direct or indirect) to the goods or services being exchanged, or that they may be being 'dumped' (offered at a price below cost). It is also very easy (and entirely rational) to conclude that the more developed countries possess an enormous in-built competitive advantage on account of their much higher levels of income (GDP) per head of population sustained over many years. Because of the much greater capacity to tax and the higher level of domestic savings which stem from this advantage they have been enabled over decades to develop:

- vastly superior infrastructure, both physical (public utilities, transport and communications) and social (health care, education and welfare support) to what is affordable in nearly all developing countries;
- much larger capital markets with consequently much readier availability of investment finance for enterprises;
- much better access to advanced technology and management know-how (constantly reinforced by their ability to attract the most able and talented individuals from developing countries with far more attractive terms than can ever be found in the latter).

To some extent these very real inequalities in the trading relationship between rich and poor countries are implicitly recognized in the General Agreement on Tariffs and Trade (GATT), which has for over fifty years formed the basis of the international trade system and is now subsumed under the World Trade Organization (WTO). In particular Article XVIII of GATT permits developing countries to introduce higher tariffs as a means of protecting 'infant industries'. Yet this has not prevented the US (with at least tacit support from the European Union) from pressurizing developing countries to engage in substantial opening of their markets to imports – as a condition either of their joining the WTO (formed in 1995) or of receiving aid from the IMF or World Bank.

Indeed the establishment of the WTO has only served to underline the fundamental impossibility of creating the 'level playing field' which so many governments and transnational corporations ritually claim to be seeking. Thus for all the insistence of its advocates that it constitutes a 'rules-based' system, experience has regularly shown that while, as in the past, large and powerful trading nations or blocs such the US, Japan and the EU can all too easily flout rulings of the WTO disputes panels which they do not like – or postpone implementing them more or less indefinitely – smaller nations are easily coerced into compliance.

The possibility that these basic imbalances between rich, well-endowed and powerful countries on the one hand and the poor and impotent on the other could be eliminated is clearly unimaginable even in the most remote long term. Hence the notion that free trade between rich and poor countries can ever be fair is patently false. Still more fundamentally, however, it should by now be obvious that, even if the playing field could by some miracle be levelled, responsible governments cannot be expected to accept the consequences of even undistorted competition where this can be seen as potentially causing social damage or waste of resources.

HYPOCRISY IN ACTION: THE EXAMPLE OF FREE TRADE IN AGRICULTURE

Nowhere has the gap between the rhetoric of the well-financed free trade lobby and the reality of systematic market distortion been better demonstrated than in the field of agriculture. In fact this sector is one which throughout most of the post-World War II period has been regarded by the governments of all industrialized market economies as a special case, justifying not only protection of national farm industries against imports but a significant degree of state intervention to stabilize domestic markets for key food products. The well-known reasons for adopting this position, which many leading agricultural economists have nevertheless appeared conveniently to forget in recent years, are that:

- Agricultural markets are naturally prone to extreme cyclical fluctuations in the supply and price of commodities, on account of (i) the involvement of large numbers of producers each taking autonomous annual decisions on varying the pattern and volume of their output, and (ii) the uncertain impact of climate and disease;
- Agriculture is a sector of strategic importance to any country, requiring the maintenance of a minimum level of self-sufficiency in essential foodstuffs.

Hence in order to limit the damaging impact of sharp price variations on both producers and consumers and at the same time avoid undue dependence on imports it has been considered appropriate for governments to intervene in commodity markets through various mechanisms (including buying up surplus stocks). Indeed so compelling were these arguments perceived to be in the post-war era that it was decided in 1950, largely at the behest of the United States, that the GATT rules should not apply to agriculture.

  It is unquestionably true that many of the official schemes of agricultural support practised by OECD countries since 1950 have been characterized by a high degree of waste and the subsidizing of chronic overproduction, the most conspicuous instance being the European Common Agricultural Policy. Hence, even though such intervention did achieve an important measure of market stability, it did so at a cost to taxpayers which they found increasingly irksome (especially as those engaged in farming constituted a small and dwindling minority of the workforce). At the same time it also caused international friction as a result of the distorting impact of surpluses being dumped on world markets.

It is thus not altogether surprising that, as the ideological tide favouring market liberalization swept the world from the early 1980s, agriculture was seen as a priority target by the vast majority of political parties in the industrial market economies. At the same time agriculture was brought under the rules of GATT's successor (the WTO) and suddenly proclaimed to be no different to manufacturing or any other sector, not least by the US authorities. For the latter perceived that, in contrast to the position in 1950, the US farm sector – together with the politically influential agrochemical industry – had now acquired a competitive edge, with the benefit of decades of taxpayer support, that would enable it to capture a substantial share of global markets.

By the mid-1990s this *volte face* may have seemed to be vindicated, as levels of farm subsidy in the OECD countries were enabled to decline in line with rising world prices for most cereals and correspondingly adequate farm incomes. However, once this price boom had stimulated the predictable cyclical response of overproduction it was inevitable that prices would fall again. But instead of sticking to their new-found faith in free agricultural markets, the US and other governments responded to the collapse in prices by renewing high levels of support to bail out their beleaguered farmers. Hence by 1999 the proportion of farm incomes in OECD countries estimated to be accounted for by official support measures, which had fallen from 40 per cent in 1990 to around 30 per cent in 1996, had shot up to 40 per cent again[11] and by the end of 2000 was reported to have reached 50 per cent in the US.[12]

Undaunted by this spectacular, albeit little noticed, failure of neo-liberal ideology, the Clinton administration continued to impose this destructive dogma on the world's poorest countries as a condition of continued economic aid. Thus in 2000 the IMF was still insisting that Haiti, one of the world's very poorest countries, open its markets to imports of subsidized rice from the US as a condition for receiving desperately needed IMF loan support. The result was that many Haitian farmers, unable to compete, were induced to risk their own and their families' lives as 'boat people' seeking illegal entry to the US, with a high proportion drowning in the attempt.[13] Moreover, as a visit to any British supermarket today can testify, subsidized US rice exports have been allowed to drive supplies from other leading exporters (including developing country producers such as Thailand which would otherwise be highly competitive) almost completely off the shelves. Such market-distorting practices have also, be it noted, contributed greatly to the long-term decline in the world prices not only of rice but of nearly all major agricultural commodities, most of which in 2000 averaged not more than half the level recorded in 1980 after allowing for inflation (i.e. in constant US dollars).[14] This decline has been exacerbated, moreover, by World Bank support for overexpansion of output of many commodities – notably of coffee in Vietnam in the 1990s, with disastrous consequences for producer prices all over the world.[15]

DEREGULATION AND ANARCHY

In view of these stark realities the attempt by rich nations to persuade poorer ones that 'free' trade can benefit them amounts to a big lie, acceptance of which can only further disadvantage the latter, even assuming they were to be granted greater access to the markets of the former. Equally harmful, it should be stressed, has been the enforced deregulation of international capital flows since the 1970s, which has enabled major western corporations and financial institutions to move money across frontiers at will. In the process they are able to use their huge financial muscle (relative to the average size of Third World economies) to extract important tax and other concessions from the national governments concerned, while feeling no restraint on their ability to withdraw their funds without warning. The potentially dire consequences of such behaviour were graphically demonstrated in the financial crises in Mexico (1994–95) and East Asia (1997–98), which led to sharp and highly disruptive falls in the exchange rate, widespread bank insolvency and millions of job losses in all the countries affected.

In continuing to advocate (however hypocritically) a free-for-all in world trade, the global capitalist establishment is seeking to distract attention from other equally damaging distortions of the present system which affect developed and developing economies alike. Indeed these problems, which have now become a particular focus of public attention (as notably expressed by protestors at the WTO meeting in Seattle in 1999), go beyond technical issues of fair competition to the fundamental political and social concerns that underlie them. These relate above all to the following issues.

Labour standards and human rights

It has been enshrined in international agreements for many years that the adoption of minimum standards for the treatment of workers and respect for their rights is a desirable policy for all countries. These standards are defined in the conventions of the International Labour Organization (the oldest of the UN specialist agencies)[16] and are reinforced by provisions of the UN Declaration of Human Rights relating to freedom of association. Despite this and the fact that the GATT/WTO has for so long promoted the merits of the international exchange of goods and services based on free but fair competition, it is far from universally recognized that the application of similar labour standards by individual states should be a condition of trade between them. On the contrary, it is generally considered that cheap labour is one of the few competitive advantages (if not the only one) possessed by most developing countries in relation to the otherwise much more favourably endowed countries of the industrialized world, and that nothing should be done to diminish it. Hence it is argued (particularly by many Third World governments) that any attempt to impose the same requirements for treatment of labour as prevail in the OECD countries is actually a form of protectionism. Thus they insist that developing countries should be permitted, for example, to put restraints on the right of workers to organize in trade unions and to apply only the lightest regulation of health and safety standards for employees.

It comes as no surprise to find that OECD governments are extremely ambivalent about such deviation from international norms by Third World states, given that like the latter they are often all too beholden to the transnational corporate interests which are the main beneficiaries of such licence to exploit labour. Indeed, while some OECD governments (such as the Clinton administration in the US) have felt obliged to give verbal endorsement to the complaints of their domestic trade unions against what they reasonably see as departures from fair trade principles, they have as often been inclined to lower their own labour standards. Thus notably in Britain in the 1980s the Thatcher administration effectively reneged on the country's long-standing commitment to ILO conventions concerning the right to strike and freedom of association when it outlawed 'secondary action' by trade union groups, an action which the Labour government in power since 1997 has declined to reverse.

Environmental protection

As concern has grown since the 1970s over the damaging effects of many kinds of economic activity on the natural environment, there has been regulatory pressure on production industries, particularly in developed countries, to curb the polluting effects of their operations and make good any environmental damage they may have caused. Understandably, businesses have tended to react to this trend by taking steps to minimize any potential increase in their costs that might result. In a world where at the same time barriers to the free movement of goods and investment capital have been coming down they have naturally tended to consider relocating their operations to countries where controls are less strict as a cost-effective option.

As in the case of regulation of labour standards, the implications for attempts to assure free and fair international trade are obvious. Countries which are willing and able to pursue a lax regime of environmental protection, which often turn out to be the ones which also have little regard for workers' rights, find that this adds to their attraction for the footloose investment of transnational corporations. By the same token attempts to use such abuses as grounds for trade discrimination, most commonly against developing countries, are also typically claimed to be protectionist, especially as there is for the most part only a very weak basis for asserting the existence of international standards. Such claims gain added force when it is pointed out that the developed country interest groups calling for such discrimination come from countries which are themselves the source of many times more pollution per head of population than emanates from any Third World country.

Taxation

Unlike the position in respect of labour and environmental regulation, there has never to date been any serious attempt to propose global standards in respect of taxation to which all countries should ideally adhere. Indeed it has long been implicitly accepted that the setting of differential tax rates, particularly in respect of direct taxation (i.e. on personal income or corporate profits), is an entirely proper and legitimate mechanism for use by countries seeking to enhance their international competitiveness. By the same token, the granting of selective tax holidays or other exemptions to encourage investment from abroad has long been accepted as normal, if not positively encouraged, by organizations such as the IMF and the OECD, notwithstanding its obviously distorting impact on market forces. This toleration of tax competition went so far as to permit the growth of an increasing number of international tax havens (or 'offshore' financial centres) in a number of (mainly small) countries from the 1960s.[17] However, in the frenetic climate of financial deregulation which has accompanied the process of globalization since the 1970s the number of such centres has doubled, reaching 128 by 1997. Belatedly, the authorities in the major industrialized countries have recognized that this proliferation constitutes a threat to the economic health and stability of the vast majority of states which practise 'normal' tax regimes. This is not only because these centres are causing them an increasingly serious loss of tax revenues through illegal tax evasion, but because the large degree of secrecy which is afforded to those who make use of these offshore facilities also helps perpetrators of other crimes (including fraud, corruption and drug trafficking) to cover their tracks.

By the late 1990s the situation was perceived to be so dangerously
out of control that the OECD itself, for so long the principal architect and promoter of globalization, was moved to begin a sustained
initiative 'to secure the integrity of tax systems by addressing the
issues raised by practices with respect to mobile activities that unfairly erode the tax bases of other countries and distort the location
of capital and services'.[18] At the same time, however, the view has
persisted among the global establishment that a 'reasonable' degree of
tax competition is healthy.[19] Not surprisingly in view of such ambivalence, most of the countries harbouring tax havens that have been
targeted by OECD attempts to make their regulatory regimes more
transparent and compliant with the requirements of the major industrialized countries (which constitute the OECD's membership)
have resisted such blatantly hypocritical demands. Such a reaction is
all the more understandable in that many of the states concerned,
notably small island economies in the Caribbean and the Pacific,
have little alternative means of attracting foreign capital or expanding
their economic base. In any case, given that the vast majority of
national governments everywhere, heavily influenced as they are by
big business, are unwilling even to discuss the possibility of international tax harmonization, it is clear the whole exercise is no more
than a gesture towards trying to check the proliferation of tax havens
and the resulting erosion of tax bases everywhere. The emptiness of
this gesture is underlined by the fact that the OECD has neither the
legal authority nor the material resources to enforce the imposition
of sanctions against any of the states it deems not to be in compliance with its arbitrary definition of 'fair' tax competition.

It is thus self-evident that the impact of global liberalization of
the kind that has been unleashed in the late twentieth century has
been to intensify a competitive lowering of standards, or 'a race to
the bottom', in respect of these vital issues of labour standards,
environmental protection and taxation. Indeed the belated moves by
the OECD to check harmful tax competition, referred to above,
demonstrate that the international ruling élite itself recognizes this
damaging reality. However, the same initiative has also exposed the
impotence of national or international authorities to take any effective

remedial action as long as they remain committed to upholding the more or less untrammelled right of private corporations to trade internationally and play off national governments against each other.

It is nevertheless apparent that growing awareness of the contradictions involved in seeking to secure the supposed benefits of liberalization while at the same time meeting the minimum requirements of economic, social and environmental security are starting to force a rethink of the whole concept of globalization. Although the strength and resilience of the forces sustaining the present anarchic order should not be underestimated, it is difficult to imagine that the contradictions and symptoms of breakdown described above will not soon compel the abandonment of the GATT/WTO regime in favour of one that:

- places more emphasis on cooperation rather than competition among nation states;
- promotes integration rather than continuation of the principle of 'sovereign independence', which remains the cornerstone of the United Nations charter and most other international agreements.

The WTO in principle discourages economic integration between nation states in that it theoretically requires that members practise non-discrimination in trade – that is, that they accord equal treatment to all other countries which are parties to the agreement. Although Article XXIV of the GATT does permit the formation of customs unions and free trade areas such as the European Union and NAFTA, there is no doubt that its bias is against such arrangements. As such it may be said to have inhibited the development of effective regional integration in the Third World, thereby preventing the many small and poor countries in the world from taking effective steps to overcome their inherent handicap of having limited domestic markets and weak national currencies.

To Third World eyes such restrictions, taken together with the very limited scope under the GATT rules for poor countries to apply greater protection to their domestic markets, doubtless strengthen the traditional perception of international trade as a mercantilist struggle between nation states for a share of world markets, a struggle, moreover, in which the odds are stacked in favour of the rich countries. This view is further reinforced by the recognition that these global markets are in any case both limited in relation to the exponential growth in world-wide productive capacity and (under capitalism) highly unstable, thereby providing a recurrent source of social insecurity and international conflict.

Another consequence of global free trade which is starting to be perceived as damaging is that it has the effect of stimulating often wasteful and environmentally damaging transfers of goods between different parts of the world, which are all the more regrettable where this results from subsidies and other market distortions. Thus trade flows involving, for example, the transport of cloth thousands of kilometres from western Europe to the former Soviet bloc to be made up into garments and then shipped back again for sale in western Europe are only commercially viable because of: (i) subsidies to road haulage by EU governments; and (ii) inadequate labour standards applied in the east European countries. Indeed it is hard to see how such exchanges could be equated with economic efficiency, especially in view of the greater pollution and road congestion that results but which is obviously not reflected in the costs and prices of the products concerned.

It may be concluded from the evidence presented in this chapter that decades of applying the supposedly liberal principles of GATT/ WTO have not only failed to bring about anything that could even begin to merit the description of global free trade; they have instead created a world of increasing imbalances and competitive anarchy in which the strong can impose themselves on the weak by means of ever greater distortions of market forces. Given the failure of this 'system' to deliver prosperity or security to more than a rather small minority of the world's people, it may well also be concluded that, since some such distortion has been shown to be inevitable, it might as well be applied in a way that may bring greater stability and equity than the GATT/WTO model can ever hope to do.

Thus, in a world where: (i) 'free and fair' international competition is inherently unattainable; and (ii) attempts to promote it are to an increasing extent counter-productive in relation to the wider interests of the world community, an alternative model is required. This will have to be based on acceptance of the following broad principles:

1. *More cooperation, less competition*   Greater emphasis will need to be placed on cooperation rather than competition in international trade. This would mean more explicit management of trade flows – whether on a bilateral or multilateral basis – so as to provide some guarantees of security for suppliers and users alike (including reasonable price stability). Such agreements should be re-negotiable every few years and subject to compliance with both agreed quality standards and appropriate labour and environmental standards.

2. *Protection of weaker economies*   The poorest and weakest countries and regions of the world must be enabled to protect their econo-mies to a sufficient degree to ensure that they can reduce the enormous gap in living conditions between themselves and the rich industrialized nations. This would mean allowing, or indeed encouraging, the more disadvantaged countries to pursue an ap-propriate degree of national or regional self-sufficiency.

3. *Economic integration*   The bias in favour of 'non-discriminatory free trade' must be replaced with one that positively promotes greater economic integration between nation states.

Strikingly, signs of a world-wide interest in more discriminatory trade relations have begun to emerge in recent years. Thus in spite, or perhaps because, of the powerful pressures on countries to conform to the principles of global non-discriminatory free trade enshrined in GATT/WTO a growing trend has developed in the 1990s towards creating structures of international exchange based on bilateral or regional cooperation. Thus the number of bilateral or regional trade agreements quadrupled between 1995 and 2001, to around 400.[20]

It is of course implicit in the idea of greater economic integration among nations that they must accept a steadily increasing degree of harmonization of standards in matters which affect the level of eco-nomic activity and competitiveness. Equally, emphasizing cooperation as much as or more than competition implies developing structures to facilitate the cost-effective transfer of resources from the wealthier to the less advantaged countries and regions (as already happens within the European Union and many of the individual richer nation states). The deficiencies of the existing global order in this respect, rooted in long-standing traditions of imperialism as well as in the inherently dysfunctional profits system, are described in Chapter 5.

Box 4.1 *New structures for world trade: cooperation, not competition*

- Increasing emphasis on managed trade flows based on fixed-term, renegotiable agreements (bilateral or multilateral);
- Poor and disadvantaged countries or regions must be enabled to protect their own markets in the interests of closing the gap in living standards with the developed world;
- 'Non-discrimination' in international trade should be de-emphasized so as to permit greater economic and political integration between nation states;
- Maximum localization of trade flows (limiting excessive transport costs and potential damage to the environment) except where 'scale economies' (e.g. petroleum refining) favour large units supplying wide areas.

CHAPTER 5

THE CRISIS OF
UNDERDEVELOPMENT:
SEARCHING FOR A NEW MODEL

As described in earlier chapters, the half century or so since World War II has witnessed both the decolonization of most of the world's less developed countries and a conspicuous failure to close the huge gap in living standards between them and the industrialized market economies. Indeed the available statistical evidence indicates that while this gap was more or less stable during the 1960s and 1970s, it actually widened significantly in the 1980s and 1990s. Thus whereas between 1960 and 1980 average income (measured as Gross National Product per head of population) in the industrial market economies fluctuated between 16 and 18 times more than the average level in the 'low and middle-income' economies, by the late 1990s this ratio had risen to 22–23:1.[1]

Moreover, it is evident that much of the population in the poor countries has experienced an absolute decline in living standards since 1980. For even though statistically income per head has continued to record a slight average increase, the huge income disparities within most developing countries and the impact of growing budgetary deficits and debt burdens on their already minuscule welfare services (health and education notably) have pushed hundreds of millions into ever more intense deprivation.

This growing inequality between rich and poor nations, which reflects a combination of slightly lower aggregate economic growth and much higher population growth in the less developed countries over the period, is in fact a continuation or recurrence of trends discernible since the start of the twentieth century.[2] What makes its persistence particularly disturbing at the end of the century, however, is that this has happened in spite of the world community having, for the first time in history, taken conscious steps to try and close the gap. For since the 1950s the industrial market economies, acting separately and through multilateral bodies such as the World Bank and various United Nations agencies, have devoted significant resources to 'development aid' with the avowed objective of raising the living standards of the poor, or less developed, countries (also commonly referred to as the Third World) closer to those of the industrialized nations. Ironically, the main (if not the only) positive achievement of development aid has arguably been to reduce the incidence of famine and the rate of peri-natal mortality, thereby increasing life expectancy and accelerating the rate of population growth in many countries (at least up to the 1980s). However, because this boost to the population has not occurred (as it did in nineteenth-century Europe) in conjunction with a commensurate rise in the demand for labour, it has merely served to exacerbate the gap in living standards with the increasingly static populations of the developed world.

The ultimate failure of this development effort to prevent a renewed widening of the gap – after some respite in the 1950s and 1960s – thus raises fundamental questions about the capacity of the present world economic order to bring about any mitigation of this growing global inequality. The main phases of the steady decline in the fortunes of the developing world since the 1950s, which largely mirrors the broader long-term deterioration in the global economy as a whole, are summarized in Box 5.1 overleaf.

The need to confront the problems raised by this chronic failure, for so long treated by the western global establishment as one of its lesser policy priorities, has by the start of the new century become inescapable. This is because, after decades in which the creeping economic paralysis of the Third World has either been ignored or wished away in clouds of hype about the bright prospects for 'emerging markets', the reality of civil breakdown in many poor countries has finally begun to threaten the developed countries themselves. The most immediate symptom of this danger is the reported tenfold

Box 5.1   *The fading dream of development 1950–2000*

- *Dashed hopes of take-off*   The optimism of the initial post-independence phase, when the prospect of achieving self-sustaining growth still seemed plausible, was blown apart in the early 1970s by the collapse of the post-war global boom.

- *Decline into debt slavery, 1974–82*   The onset of world recession (combined with inflation) left many less developed countries (LDCs) with serious external imbalances, particularly where they were dependent on imports of petroleum, whose price was suddenly increased fourfold by the Organization of Petroleum Exporting Countries (OPEC). Nevertheless for a brief period western bankers were encouraged to lend large sums to LDCs, apparently on the assumption that all commodity exporters were about to emulate OPEC and become rich thanks to rising world prices (there was in fact a brief speculative commodity price boom in the mid-1970s). The resulting orgy of corrupt lending, mainly for projects which were manifestly non-viable, or even non-existent, came to an end with Mexico's declaration of insolvency in 1982. By this time most other LDCs had also accrued debts they were quite incapable of servicing.

- *'Structural adjustment', liberalization, stagnation and collapse* Faced with worsening structural deficits, poor countries were forced into drastic measures to cut public spending in order to try and contain their growing arrears on debt service. At the same time aid donors, led by the IMF and World Bank, insisted on the removal of restraints to the free movement of goods and capital as a condition of further financial support. The result was that most LDCs were progressively less able to protect or subsidize their industries in the face of stronger overseas competitors, leading them into a vicious circle of slowing growth, still greater indebtedness, declining public services, capital flight and currency weakness. The only countries which were able (for a while) to avoid this disaster were those few, mainly in East Asia, that were enabled, or even encouraged, to protect and subsidize their export-oriented industries. Once the supposed 'miracle' of these and other 'emerging markets' had dissolved in the face of growing global financial turmoil in the late 1990s the so-called tiger economies faced almost as grim a prospect as the rest of the Third World.

rise since the 1980s in the numbers of refugees and asylum seekers (including many from the equally afflicted countries of the collapsed former Soviet bloc) trying to enter the European Union – not to mention a comparable upsurge in the number of would-be illegal immigrants seeking to enter the United States across the Mexican border. Meanwhile, back in the blighted countries from which they are fleeing, particularly in Africa and Latin America, groups of the economically dispossessed resort to increasingly desperate acts of protest and plunder (including appalling atrocities) in an effort both to survive and to force the world to take notice of them.[3]

THE BANKRUPTCY OF CONVENTIONAL MODELS OF DEVELOPMENT

Both the reasons and the various suggested remedies for the Third World's persistently low level of development have been the subject of a vast amount of research and debate over the decades. Indeed, as noted by the World Bank in 2000, 'Development thinking has followed a circuitous path over the past 50 years. At various times it has emphasized market failures and market successes, governments as active interventionists or passive enablers, openness to trade, saving and investment, education, financial stability, the spread of knowledge, macroeconomic stability, and more'.[4] Yet in the same report the Bank is forced to concede there is no evidence that any of the conventional approaches that have been tried can offer a viable way out of the Third World's chronic predicament.

Indeed the reality of the failure of all the mainstream models of development that have been followed since World War II is now having to be confronted by their various advocates. Proponents of the traditional approach based on transfers of aid have been forced to concede that it has not only failed to generate self-sustaining growth in developing countries but has too often been a stimulus to waste, corruption and unserviceable debt burdens, much as many critics on the *laissez-faire* right always claimed that it would.[5] However, the latter for their part have also now witnessed the demonstrable bankruptcy of their revisionist approach based on deregulation and liberalization. Indeed, as already noted, the purported revival of free market economic policies has been largely a sham everywhere, as governments in thrall to big business have been unable to avoid increasing resort to corporate welfare and other forms of market distortion in order to assure minimum levels of stability. It could be pointed out, moreover, that, had the free market school sincerely believed in its own propaganda it would have sought to phase out development aid altogether. In reality, such a drastic move has never been contemplated. Moreover, one of the few official bodies to advance half-way serious proposals for reform of development aid in recent years, reporting to the US Congress in 2000, has contented itself with advocating that more funds be channelled through or managed by the private sector.[6]

The inability of either of these major strands of mainstream thinking to address the fundamental problems of the developing world is thus becoming more and more conspicuous, as is the danger to international stability caused by the failure of the global establishment to develop a more realistic strategy. However, the ruling élite is precluded from considering any alternative approach which might involve a radical deviation either from the neo-liberal economic ideology favoured by Washington or from the traditional pattern of political relations between the industrialized and developing countries.

The reasons for the refusal of the ruling global establishment seriously to address the fundamental weaknesses of the economic order have already been spelt out. At the political level, it has also been suggested that the relationship between the developed and developing nations since most of the latter were decolonized between 1945 and 1970 has changed remarkably little since before political 'independence' (particularly in Africa and Latin America). In most cases, indeed, the only difference is that hegemony is now exercised mainly by the United States, albeit generally with the full acquiescence of the former European colonial powers and other OECD governments. Yet it is apparent both that this neo-imperialist model of world order is becoming increasingly untenable and that the reluctance of the US and its allies to confront this failure is creating further obstacles to the resolution of the wider global economic crisis.

THE ILLUSION OF NATIONAL INDEPENDENCE

One of the central implicit assumptions of the post-World War II order which still remains the basis of international relations is that politically the world is, or should be, composed of nation states which are sovereign within their own borders. Hence the process of decolonization which brought the vast majority of United Nations member states into existence has proceeded on the assumption that, in nearly every case,[7] former colonies will attain the status of nationhood once the colonial power formally gives up sovereignty. Likewise it has also been generally understood that, once independent, these new nations will assume full responsibility for their own destinies, including providing for their own basic material needs. This is true notwithstanding the incidence of a considerable number of obvious exceptions to this rule, comprising mainly states which were regarded at independence as manifestly too small or lacking in resources to be capable of meaningful economic self-sufficiency, at least in anything like the foreseeable future. Such entities, most of which are small island economies in the Caribbean or the Pacific and Indian Oceans, have commonly been set up on the basis of a special economic relationship with the former colonial power, which typically undertakes to provide some form of grant-in-aid to help finance the administration for a more or less indefinite period.

Unfolding events since the 1960s have revealed that this handicap of being endowed from the outset with a seriously inadequate economic base has by no means been confined to the smallest states. Thus by 1998 Uganda, a fairly typical country of sub-Saharan Africa with a population of 21 million, had an aggregate Gross National Product roughly equal in size to that of a British city of 300,000 inhabitants such as Coventry.[8] Even allowing for some distortion in such comparative data, these indicators of relative economic size, which apply to most other poor countries and in general have changed little in the 30 years or more since decolonization, are a telling reflection of the difficulties confronting the majority of states in the Third World in trying to exercise their 'sovereign independence'. For it is not hard to see that economies which are so small, relative to the size of their populations, have severely restricted capacity to mobilize enough tax revenues to finance the minimum level of institutions and infrastructure needed to enable a modern state to function, including roads, education, health, defence, law enforcement and a reasonably incorruptible civil service. The inadequacy of the tax base compared with more developed countries is, moreover, magnified by the low level of average incomes and the large proportion of economic activity which takes place outside the formal economy, so that the proportion of taxpayers in the total population is extremely small.

It may be true that the chronic inability of most former colonies to achieve or maintain a reasonable degree of economic self-sufficiency was not foreseen at the time of independence. Yet the fact that it clearly was recognized in the case of those territories where continued dependence after decolonization was provided for raises the question of why greater care was not taken before independence to consider how the viability of most newly independent states was to be assured. There seem in fact to have been a number of factors favouring a hasty process of decolonization without profound consideration of the long-term economic implications for the new states:

1. International political pressures against colonialism were strong in the aftermath of World War II and were expressed with steadily increasing vigour at the United Nations, while Cold War propaganda considerations were also a factor.
2. The demand for independence within the colonial territories themselves was growing at the same time, particularly among the western-educated local élites who stood to inherit the key positions of power.
3. Domestic pressures within the colonial powers increasingly reflected embarrassment at the continued imperial relationship, particularly as the price of maintaining control, in terms of blood as well as money, began to mount.
4. Most such territories were perceived as a wasting economic asset from the standpoint of the colonial powers, all the more so because the wealth they once derived from such possessions had progressively dwindled as: (i) their ability to exploit labour had progressively declined (ever since the abolition of slavery or indentured labour); and (ii) the value of their traditional export commodities (such as cane sugar) had likewise steadily diminished.[9] Perhaps it was growing awareness of such economic fragility that made local leaders of some of the later candidates for decolonization (in the 1970s) reluctant to accept independence, so that they were only induced to do so by the offer of a substantial fiscal endowment from the departing colonial authority.[10]

If such were indeed the attitudes conditioning the drive to decolonization, there must clearly be doubt as to how far the commitment of the rich countries to raising the living standards of the poor countries in general was genuine and meaningful. Is it not in fact more plausible to suppose that the policy of the governments of developed nations (whether or not they were former colonial powers) was driven by far more self-interested motives? These almost certainly comprised

- a desire to avoid the increasingly onerous cost, both political and financial, of governing territories which held out less promise of yielding commercial benefits to the metropolis than had previously seemed to be the case, but where pressure for improvements in the lot of the inhabitants (e.g. in education) were becoming inescapable;
- concern to retain as much influence as possible over the governments of the newly independent countries, particularly in respect of decisions that might affect developed country interests, whether corporate or strategic.

Indeed the behaviour of the former colonial powers seems to confirm the suspicion that the dominant western countries were at best indifferent to the weakness of Third World states arising from the small size of their economies, and even in some cases actively sought to promote it. Thus successive French governments of the 1950s promoted the fragmentation of their two giant possessions of West and Equatorial Africa into a large number of small states in the run-up to independence, with the evident intention of weakening them.[11] Likewise, the British Conservative administration of 1970–74, by its active support for the military overthrow of the government of Uganda in 1971, paved the way for the break-up of the East African Community (comprising also Kenya and Tanzania), thus helping to perpetuate division and weakness in that region.

In short, there seems to be no evidence (apart from rhetoric) to support the view that the global establishment ever considered the closing of the wealth gap between the industrialized and developed countries as a high priority concern. That is not to say that there were not many, at least up to the 1970s, who sincerely believed that this was both a feasible and a desirable goal. Likewise it seemed plausible to expect, especially in the light of the successful revival of the west European economy on the back of Marshall Aid after 1948, that financial aid flows to the developing economies could enable them to achieve 'self-sustaining growth' in the foreseeable future. However, it is clear, if only with the benefit of hindsight, that the world's major economic powers were never prepared to make significant sacrifices in order that the less developed countries could enhance their economic self-sufficiency.

Indeed it is entirely consistent with the facts to conclude, as President Kwame Nkrumah of Ghana and other critics of the west did quite early in the post-independence era, that the policy of the industrialized countries towards the Third World was essentially neo-colonialist. On this interpretation, from the perspective of the departing colonial powers and the rest of the developed world, decolonization was no more than a ploy to achieve more cost-effective domination of their former empires. Indeed, as in the case of the British imperial model of indirect rule in the former princely states of India, it enabled them to exercise a large measure of continuing influence over the supposedly independent governments of developing countries while distancing themselves from responsibility for their failures and abuses.

Another measure of the lack of concern on the part of the colonial powers to leave behind genuinely independent states that were robust politically and economically is that they made little effort to ensure that the new national entities were reasonably homogeneous either ethnically or socially. Arguably this failing was largely inevitable, especially in view of the powerful pressures on them to depart as soon as possible – not least from the indigenous élites anxious to get their hands on the levers of power. It was at all events to be a crucial factor behind the subsequent discord and instability in many Third World countries, exacerbating their in-built economic fragility.

THE LEGACY OF NEO-IMPERIALISM

Whether through negligence or design, therefore, the world has inherited a post-colonial political structure in the Third World which places nominal power in the hands of national governments that for the most part are structurally incapable of mobilizing the necessary resources to run a modern state. Yet even if this was not the result of the global establishment's determination to perpetuate the economic dependency of the colonial era, the rich nations have manifestly been unwilling even to recognize the severity of this constraint, let alone do anything serious to address it. Throughout the long years of the Cold War, the US and its allies were quite happy to exploit the inherent weakness of Third World countries in pursuit of their own narrow political and corporate interests. Indeed the record of sustained western-sponsored subversion, manipulation, corruption and repression of human rights in all parts of the Third World over the last 50 years is well documented.[12]

But while this policy may have served the short-term purpose of containing forces deemed hostile to US and related western interests, it did so at very high long-term cost, both political and economic. For by effectively discouraging the emergence either of anything resembling genuinely representative government in the Third World or of a sustained general improvement in the material conditions of most of its inhabitants, the west virtually guaranteed the eventual outbreak of widespread disaffection and instability. Moreover, by its sustained support for and reliance on the most corrupt and brutal autocrats, such as Suharto in Indonesia, Mobutu in Zaire/Congo and Somoza in Nicaragua, to name but a few, the US and its allies have contrived both to undermine their own moral authority in the Third World and progressively to weaken their ability to influence events.

Thus it was inevitable that dictators who owed their position to the US or other western patrons would demand ever greater indulgence and favours, including the right to siphon off massive percentages of IMF and other aid flows, as the price of continuing to act as the stooges of foreign powers. Yet the west's willingness to pay this price has by no means guaranteed its ability to control what Third World leaders do, especially as conditions have become progressively more unstable and the demands of the donor community for 'structural adjustment' ever more unrealistic. Moreover, the damage done to the reputation of the developed world's leadership has been compounded by its willingness to aid and abet the crimes of Third World dictators and their henchmen both before and after their overthrow. Thus, for instance, Britain and Switzerland have been willing to allow the proceeds of the egregious acts of theft by the Nigerian leader General Abacha (who died in 1998) to be deposited in their banks with no questions asked, while the US and most European countries are generally quite prepared to grant the right of abode to almost any foreign national in possession of a large amount of money.

But the single most catastrophic error of the western power élite in this shameful history of betrayal and self-delusion has been to continue insisting that virtually all nominally sovereign states, however small and poor, must be deemed capable of attaining some kind of equilibrium where they will be financially self-sufficient at a tolerable standard of living. The criminal perversity of this presumption is all the greater in that it is being applied by aid donors who also insist that the countries concerned abstain from any measures that might increase their financial self-sufficiency and thereby reduce their dependence on external aid.

Thus, for example, even a very weak and notoriously disadvantaged country such as Rwanda is required by donors to withhold any protection from local agricultural and manufacturing enterprises which have a reasonable potential for competing in its home market and to give support instead to export-oriented production such as tea and coffee. However, the latter, which are essentially relics of the colonial economy, have suffered from decades of declining real prices and are hopelessly uneconomic in a country whose competitiveness in these low-value commodities is further reduced by its severely landlocked position and remoteness from export markets. Hence these crops can only be made viable, if at all, at the cost of even greater impoverishment of the population, which is already affected by chronic malnutrition. For the economy overall, therefore, this strategy only serves to stunt the growth of incomes and the ability of enterprises and individuals to pay taxes, thereby intensifying national insolvency and dependence.

THE NECESSITY OF INTERDEPENDENCE

Thus the plight of the Third World at the start of the twenty-first century provides the most graphic embodiment of the twin crises, of imperialist political control and of the capitalist economic system, referred to in Chapter 2. It has, moreover, reached a point where it is no longer possible to ignore the deficiencies of the post-war, post-decolonization structure of international relations based on the presumption of national sovereignty and independence.

Clearly any moves to address this fundamental weakness of the current world order will need to be based on the recognition that most nations cannot continue to be treated as politically independent entities which are solely responsible for their own security, whether military or economic. Rather there is a need to establish the principle of permanent interdependence between rich and poor regions of the planet enshrined in some form of binding structure. Such an arrangement is clearly implied by the proposal made as long ago as 1980 by the distinguished Brandt Commission on International Development (chaired by Willy Brandt, the former West German chancellor) for a permanent flow of financial support from rich to poor countries.[13] In fact the same principle is already extensively applied within countries or regions of the developed world to compensate permanently disadvantaged regions. This is true both in the European Union, where remote areas such as Sicily and the Western Isles of Scotland benefit from the Structural and Cohesion Funds created for this purpose, and in the US, where substantial federal funds have been deployed to support urban regeneration and subsidize enterprise in the more deprived regions of the country. It is perhaps in the same spirit that the recent US Congress advisory commission on the role of the international financial institutions recommended that henceforth the World Bank should concentrate on providing de facto subsidies to basic social services in the poorest countries, all in the form of grants rather than loans.[14]

Already, moreover, the donor community is being forced to adopt such an approach in respect of the poorest Third World countries, if only to stave off the imminent threat of total social breakdown. This is reflected in the tendency, increasingly apparent since the mid-1990s, for them to become directly involved in financing the provision of basic public services such as health and education by bankrupt Third World states, particularly the most chronically destitute African ones, such as Rwanda, Sierra Leone and Zambia. Yet perhaps the most significant application of the Brandt Commission proposal has been the long-term commitment of the United States, in place since the late 1970s, to provide food aid to Egypt. This little-publicized arrangement is also perhaps the most striking example of the linkage between aid and US neo-imperialist foreign policy. For there is no doubt the aid was originally offered by the Carter administration as part of a political deal to persuade Egypt to sign the Camp David accords with Israel in 1979, at a time when Egypt's growing structural food deficit and weak external payments position were starting to pose a serious threat to its political stability. The continuation of this arrangement to the present day is also obviously linked to continuing US foreign policy concerns in the Middle East.[15] However, in a future more democratic Egypt, whose still rapidly growing population has greatly increased its dependency on such aid since 1979, it would be bound to raise questions over the nature of the political accountability that this implies.

It is scarcely surprising that such deviations by the global establishment from the ideology of neo-liberalism have received little publicity to date. For it must obviously have occurred to the authorities in the industrialized countries that any overt moves by them to subsidize the welfare budgets of foreign countries may well provoke:

- a hostile reaction among their own public, who might wonder why their taxes are being spent on supporting social services overseas at a time when cuts in welfare benefits are being imposed at home;
- demands for similar relief in the many other poor countries still being subjected to the more rigorous fiscal discipline of traditional structural adjustment.

Such official schizophrenia is reflected in continuing attempts (evidently inspired by the US Congress) to insist that support for Third World health and education programmes be linked to the imposition of user charges even on people who have no money. On the other hand such dogmatism is often tempered in practice by greater realism within aid agencies, not least perhaps because of a recognition that the right to free minimum provision of health care and education is enshrined in the Universal Declaration of Human Rights.

The reticence of the donors on the extent of their involvement in the administration of developing countries may equally be motivated by a desire to avoid focusing attention on actions amounting to a watering-down of the principle of the sovereign independence of nation states. Indeed it might well be expected to provoke charges of neo-imperialist intervention without any consideration for the principle of democratic accountability.

Unquestionably, indeed, such moves amount to an acceptance that, whatever might be suggested by the principles of the competitive global market and sovereign independence of nation states, resources must be transferred from richer to poorer regions in order to offset 'market imperfections' and thereby maintain the minimum conditions of existence in the latter compatible with civil stability. Clearly, moreover, once the existence of such imperfections in the existing global order is conceded it may be hard to avoid pursuing such ideas to their logical conclusion.

OBSTACLES TO CHANGE

If it is accepted, as argued in these last two chapters, that it will henceforth be necessary for

1. the pattern of international trade to be determined more on the basis of cooperation than of competition;
2. the traditional boundaries of responsibility and power between nation states, which we have observed are already crumbling, to be increasingly transcended by multilateral intervention in support of the poorest and most vulnerable communities,

it is clear a radically different model of world order needs now to be envisaged. Self-evidently, however, the implications of this conclusion are profoundly threatening to the interests of the ruling élite, in the Third as well as the developed world. Hence even as the smoke-screen of bogus free-market rhetoric is blown away, continued resistance from the existing dominant vested interests to open recognition of the need for greater collectivist intervention on a global scale must be considered a certainty.

The reluctance of donor governments in general and the US in particular openly to face this reality is obviously to be explained in terms of their fear of conceding:

- the inherent inability of the competitive market model to deliver adequate living standards to large parts of the world community;
- the need for more rather than less collectivist intervention in resource allocation both within and between regions of the globe, in a way not necessarily congenial to transnational companies and the rest of the private corporate sector (the chief vested interests guiding the political process in the donor countries);
- the need to impose an increased budgetary burden on the already fiscally challenged donor countries, which again would redound to the particular disadvantage of the corporate sector.

It is thus obvious that the power élite of the industrialized world, dominated by big business interests, will constitute the crucial source of opposition to any concessions of this kind. Yet it is important to remember that strong forces of resistance to changing the status quo are also to be found among the local élites of the Third World. Indeed it is almost invariably a feature of developing countries that they have inherited a domestic social structure which is largely feudal in character and which colonial regimes had neither the desire nor the resources to change significantly during the (mostly quite brief) period of their rule. Where it did effect any change, moreover, it was often by way of encouraging the emergence of a comprador bourgeoisie from the more or less feudal landowning élite – as, for example, in the Philippines.[16] As a consequence, contrary to what the public in developed countries is often led to believe, many LDC leaders, having typically been born into a socially privileged position, are by no means enthusiastic supporters of development other than rhetorically. For, to the extent that the development process succeeds in raising the living standards of, and thereby empowering, significant numbers of poor people in developing countries, particularly in the rural areas where the majority live, it clearly tends to weaken the traditional order. Hence it is frequently found that Third World governments, few of which are subject to any meaningful democratic accountability, will seek to subvert innovations such as, for example, the establishment of autonomous peasant cooperatives which might enable impoverished rural communities to achieve genuine economic advance.[17]

Such reactionary tendencies are of course far from unwelcome to transnational corporations looking for a congenial investment location in an 'emerging' market. Indeed, they fit comfortably with the pattern of authoritarian regime, having a natural bias against anything that smacks of democracy or empowerment of the poor, that American and European interests, governmental and corporate, have long sought to foster in the Third World. Likewise it is often highly convenient for global big business to rely on the objections of developing country leaders to essential reforms (such as the application of minimum standards in the treatment of labour) sought by trade unions in developed countries, on the grounds that such demands are protectionist. Thus do such unholy alliances serve to encourage continued inaction on the part of international bodies charged with bringing about genuine reform.

It is obvious that the prevalence of such repressive governments in the vast majority of Third World countries constitutes a serious impediment to any potential moves towards the kind of redistributive intervention which is now needed to avert the further spread of disaster in these countries.

THE ONLY WAY FORWARD

We have observed how progressive economic and social breakdown in the Third World, now even affecting most of the supposed success stories of East Asia, has created ever more unbearable pressures for the world community as a whole. Likewise it has been shown how these pressures have forced the United States and its allies in the industrialized world to depart more and more from the central assumptions of the post-World War II international order so as to provide ad hoc relief of the most extreme symptoms. In so doing they have effectively conceded that: (i) most poor nation states lack the ability to fend for themselves in a competitive but unbalanced global market; and (ii) the rich countries have an obligation to intervene in bankrupt sovereign states where this is the only way to avert complete social catastrophe.

We have already noted the existence of strong vested interests biased against any such concessions to a vision of global collectivism and solidarity. But perhaps the most solid single reason for donor reluctance openly to adopt an agenda of increased transnational intervention is a more practical political one. This is the question-mark it would raise over the legitimacy of such foreign involvement in the running of supposedly independent sovereign states, that is, without any mechanisms of democratic accountability. (This dilemma is comparable to that raised by the UN's role in administering Kosovo, following the questionable war that removed it from control of the sovereign state to which it legally belongs; see Chapter 7.)

Yet the refusal of the developed nations to confront this dilemma is becoming increasingly untenable as they are drawn more deeply into direct involvement of the running of bankrupt Third World countries. This has been graphically illustrated by the recent case of Zambia, where by the late 1990s foreign donors were already financing over 30 per cent of the national budget. Yet in the face of this largesse it was still reportedly possible in 1998–99 for officials of the state mining corporation to sell a consignment of cobalt (one of the country's key exports) for US$60 million less than its market value, raising obvious suspicions of high-level theft. This was revealed, moreover, just at the time when (in early 2001) Zambia, as one of the world's poorest countries, had been granted relief on some US$4 billion of its foreign debts to the World Bank and the IMF, following a high-profile campaign in its support by international charities.[18]

It must be obvious that such intolerable abuses will not be eliminated from poor countries such as Zambia without addressing their fundamental structural and institutional weaknesses. Just as inescapably, there will need to be a progressive reordering of the present pattern of relationships between poor and rich nations, based on the corrupt exercise of power without responsibility, if a more sustainable model of development is to be attained.

It goes without saying that such a reformed model of international organization will need to be based on the principles of democratic accountability and the rule of law, and that it must in no sense entail any revival or perpetuation of imperial or quasi-imperial relationships. As such it should in principle be based on the promotion of two broad strands of integration between nation states.

1. *Creation of regional economic blocs* Poor countries would be encouraged to form groupings large enough to constitute economic entities and potential markets capable of: (i) justifying regional production of most manufactured consumer goods; and (ii) offering economies of scale in the provision of public infrastructure and services. At the same time they would be encouraged to adjust their pattern of agricultural production so as to give priority to greater self-sufficiency in basic foodstuffs. In order to ensure that these groups could thereby enhance regional economic autonomy they would be permitted under the rules of a modified WTO to discriminate against imports from third countries which might otherwise undermine the viability of local production. Likewise, as an essential condition, they would be enabled to form regional monetary blocs, buttressed by sufficient restrictions on capital flows to ensure reasonable currency stability. The overall aim would be to facilitate greater self-sufficiency and autonomy for Third World peoples *vis-à-vis* the industrialized world.

2. *More structured relations with the industrialized (donor) countries* In parallel with such close regional cooperation Third World states would be encouraged, individually or collectively, to move towards increased economic and political integration with developed states, which themselves should increasingly be formed into more tightly knit blocs (such as the European Union). Only through such structural North–South links would it be possible to create mechanisms (based on genuine democratic accountability) permitting a legitimate role for long-term aid flows from rich to poor regions of the world.

The full implications of thus moving to create the conditions in which the fragmentation and marginalization of the Third World can be ended are explored more fully in the following chapters.

Box 5.2   *Ways forward for the Third World*

- Insistence on greatly strengthening democratic institutions and popular empowerment.
- Creation of regional blocs large and strong enough to achieve a substantial measure of economic self-sufficiency, with the right to buttress this with the necessary degree of protection (including monetary autonomy) against more powerful competitive forces from outside.
- More structured involvement of developed countries, through sustained flows of aid, in the running of developing countries, based on enhanced democratic accountability on both sides.

CHAPTER 6

IN PLACE OF THE 'FREE' MARKET

The earlier chapters of this book have described how and why the global economic and political order has been reduced to a state of chronic instability and spreading misery since the early 1970s. At the same time some account has also been given of the ways in which the ruling powers are being forced, in order to preserve a minimum level of stability amid the growing chaos, to contradict their own *laissez-faire* rhetoric and revive or extend state intervention in the economy. Yet it has also been made clear that the global establishment is driven by vested interests for which any recognition of the need for a more collectivist model of world order would be fatal. Hence all western governing parties have been forced into an ever more blatant contradiction between their rhetoric glorifying the theoretical beneficence of the liberalized global market and their inescapable compulsion to distort market forces.

As noted in the Introduction, a central assumption of this work is that unavoidable systemic collapse is about to overtake global financial markets, and indeed has already begun to take hold (as of early 2001). It is further assumed that only in the event of such a systemic breakdown will the political pressure for a radical restructuring of the economic system become irresistible, bearing in mind what is at stake for the ruling élite in terms of preserving their enormous power and wealth. Taking account of such emerging political realities, therefore, the remaining chapters seek to suggest the most plausible pattern of evolution towards a more sustainable global order, both economic and political.

It will be apparent that this indicative model takes it as given that any alternative to the present world order must indeed be global in scope, indeed far more genuinely so than the present one, and that any supposed solutions based on national 'fortresses' or inward-looking regional blocs must be rejected. To anyone who doubts the necessity of this presumption it must be pointed out that:

- in a world where the population has grown threefold in the last 50 years and may double again in the next 50 it will be increasingly impossible for rich countries to isolate themselves from economically marginalized communities demanding their attention;
- environmental pressures (such as global warming and dwindling marine fish resources) can be dealt with only on an international basis.

THE INEVITABILITY OF COLLECTIVISM

The results of the so-called neo-liberal experiment which has been the dominant influence on western policy makers at least since 1980 indicate unambiguously that:

- notwithstanding the extensive liberalization and deregulation of markets which has occurred, the supposed moves to reduce the role of the state in the economy have been largely a sham;
- to the extent that the revival of *laissez-faire* has been a reality it has failed to lift the world economy out of the chronic stagnation affecting it since the 1970s or to prevent its ultimate slide into intolerable chaos.

The preceding analysis has also made clear that the principal reason for this spectacular failure, as in major capitalist collapses of the past, is the inherent dependency of the profits system on a perpetual rapid growth of markets which can never in fact be sustained beyond a relatively brief period. Now that this historic bane of capitalism has been compounded by technological changes which have effectively rendered the scarcity of funds for investment a thing of the past, it is time to develop a model of economic organization that puts capital

in its proper place. At the same time, in view of the de facto acceptance even by the defenders of the existing system that extensive
intervention in the economy by the collective[1] is an essential condition of economic stability, a frank recognition of this necessity
must replace the hypocritical pretence that it should be avoided.

Once it is recognized that collectivist intervention is needed to
remedy the inherent weaknesses of the prevailing profits system, it
will be essential to move towards an alternative model that incorpo-
rates principles and mechanisms ensuring a proper balance between
public- and private-sector interests. However, in seeking to avoid the
damaging consequences of the existing system, it will be important
to try and steer clear of the pitfalls associated with existing or previous
collectivist economic systems. In the light of these broad principles
the essential features of a more functional economic model are
described in the following pages.

DOWNGRADING OF GROWTH AS A PRIORITY

As noted above, and as underlined by the experience of the recent
past, the sustained high levels of economic growth needed to assure
the survival of the profits system are almost certainly unattainable.
For, as suggested in Chapter 2, the clear message indicated by trends
since World War II is that global economic growth rates cannot for
long significantly exceed their historic average of 2–2.5 per cent over
the long term (which is indeed in line with the average rate achieved
by the industrial market economies since 1980). At the same time,
thanks to technological change since the 1970s and the corresponding
growth in importance of intangible assets, the demand for fixed
capital investment is likely in future to grow more slowly still
compared with past trends. Consequently the problem of finding an
outlet for the reinvestment of the inexorable flow of corporate profits
will become more chronic than ever. This in turn means that, quite
contrary to what has been proclaimed by official propaganda over
the last 50 years, so far from the capitalist cycle of boom and bust
being a thing of the past, it is set to recur more frequently than ever.

It follows from this conclusion that it will be, at the very least, futile to pursue economic policies designed to maximize output growth, particularly under any form of capitalist economy. Under modern conditions, moreover, it may be positively counter-productive, in so far as:

- the resulting cyclical fluctuations of the economy will entail ever more frequent surges in demand for welfare payments and consequent destabilization of public finance;
- it tends to exacerbate pressure on the environment by boosting the incidence of harmful phenomena such as global warming.

There will thus be every reason to insist that, at least for the more developed countries, the existing bias towards maximizing economic growth be downgraded in favour of an emphasis on stability. This emphasis will in turn mean that it will no longer be admissible to argue that the huge global problem of poverty, both absolute and relative, can be solved by seeking to maximize overall economic growth, on the questionable assumption that this will push up living standards across the board. In these circumstances it will have to be recognized that the only alternative way of solving the problem is through redistribution of income and wealth, both within and between nations.

LIMITS TO PROFIT MAXIMIZATION

It has been noted that genuine competition tends to be either unattainable, wasteful or unacceptably destructive, notwithstanding the gains it may sometimes confer on consumers in the short run. To the extent that this is found to be true in any particular economic sector, therefore, public intervention will be required to compensate for any market 'imperfection', for example, through de facto subsidy or price control. A priori, however, companies which are thus specially protected by the collective should at the very least be required to conform with publicly defined standards of quality and performance and should also be obliged to submit their practices and financial records to public scrutiny. Only under such tight conditions should enterprises be permitted to pursue maximization of their profits.

Similar constraints would in principle need to be applied to enterprises enjoying any other special privileges conferred by the state, whether or not they were benefiting from extra protection from uncontrolled market forces. In particular the right to limited liability status, enabling individual shareholders or proprietors to avoid the risk of personal bankruptcy in the event of damage or losses caused to others, should no longer be granted to an enterprise unless some clear public interest in doing so can be demonstrated. This is because the principal justification for this general privilege – the need to attract large amounts of equity capital from a great number of investors having no direct involvement in running the business – is no longer the high priority it was considered to be when the right was first introduced in the 1850s. This is the result of the decline in demand for fixed capital in the modern economy due to changing technology (see Chapter 2). Moreover, the tendency for limited liability to be exploited as a cover for fraud is another reason for careful scrutiny of those who would take advantage of it.

The need in principle to impose restraints on the pursuit of profit maximization, thereby qualifying the traditional primacy of shareholders' interests under standard company law, will naturally tend to weaken the enthusiasm of investors for putting money into such businesses. This is because the potential rates of return on shares in the companies affected would be too low to counterbalance the risk of loss (or, in investors' jargon, the risk:reward ratio would be too high). This in turn would tend to mean that private investment in corporations would increasingly be in the form of debt (i.e. bearing a fixed rate of return), while the public sector would tend by default to acquire a controlling interest in the equity, thus assuming most or all of the risk. In short, by imposing an upper limit on the scope for profit maximization, the community would effectively be creating a bias in favour of public ownership of a majority of enterprises.

Ironically, one of the results of the privatization of virtually all the public utilities in Britain since 1980 has been to demonstrate that such a bias against private ownership of key industries is ultimately unavoidable. This is because the need for public regulation of these natural monopolies has led to the imposition of restraints on prices such that the return on shareholders' investment is quite modest relative to that demanded by the market. This in turn has meant, especially in the feverish investment climate of the late 1990s, that shares in the privatized utilities are unattractive both to institutional investors increasingly desperate to boost the performance of their portfolios and to speculative investors looking for a quick killing. Hence there have been growing moves by boards of directors, starting in the water supply sector from 2000, to try and divest these assets by selling them to non-profit trusts.[2] This model was preferred to an outright return to state ownership for the rather obvious reason that an overt re-nationalization of water utilities only 10 years after they had been privatized would have amounted to a politically unacceptable reversal for the British establishment, notwithstanding the fact that a supposedly social democratic government had by then replaced the dogmatically free-market Conservative administration which was responsible for the original privatization.

Such developments have in fact served to emphasize how in a country like Britain it is coming to be seen that the inherent conflict between the interests of private shareholders and those of the public in respect of essential services must ultimately to be resolved in favour of the latter, if only after considerable cost to taxpayers. Indeed, the unfolding dénouement of British water privatization, whether or not it ends in the de facto return of these utilities to public-sector control, has had the effect of calling into question the most central assumption of capitalism. This is the principle, enshrined in company law everywhere, that companies are run for the primary benefit of their shareholders, whose interests must therefore take precedence over all others. Once this assumption is removed, as increasingly is happening in the case of the British privatized utilities, the interest of private investors in assuming risk in return for what may seem scant reward is certain to wane.

Hence for those seeking to defend the status quo, under which private-sector companies have largely been left to pursue their own priorities free of state interference, the advent of privatized utilities (once viewed as a symbol of triumphant *laissez-faire* capitalism) has finally proved to be a dangerous development. For it has established the precedent that privately owned companies should be subject to state regulation where the public interest requires it. The significance of this, at a time when large corporations have come under growing public criticism for actions perceived to be harmful to the community (such as the mass closure by the major British banks of branches in rural areas in 1999–2000), should not be underestimated. Indeed there have even suggestions in the media and political circles in Britain of a need to create a public regulator for banks, supermarket chains and even the motor vehicle industry.

To the extent that this trend towards greater public restraint on companies' freedom of action is extended further it clearly can only be negative for the level of their profits. It is thus quite plausible to envisage a growing acceptance of the idea that holding down corporate profits is broadly in the public interest, particularly if it also comes to be seen that the recycling of surplus profits through the market is all too likely to promote financial instability.

Indeed more general moves to discourage, or even largely eliminate, the pursuit of profit maximization could easily come to be accepted as publicly beneficial in several respects. Among these will be the valuable side-effect of reducing the morally disfiguring distortions of the market which have become an increasingly unacceptable feature of the latter-day capitalist order. Thus it would sharply diminish the compulsion both for companies to engage in fraudulent exaggeration of their financial performance and for banks and investment institutions to succumb to the temptations of moral hazard. At the same time it would remove any possible objection to the enforcement of proper minimum standards for the remuneration and treatment of labour in an environment where the pressure to compete at all costs would disappear.

ALTERNATIVES TO THE PROFIT MOTIVE

If the drive to maximize profits is thus to be downgraded as the principal spur to enterprise and effective corporate performance, it is

IN PLACE OF THE 'FREE' MARKET   113

obviously essential to consider through what alternative mechanisms
management and workers are to be motivated. For it would be dangerous to pretend, in the light of past experience of state-owned
enterprises, that such businesses have not often suffered from a lack
of adequate incentive to perform cost-effectively and respond to the
demands of consumers.

The answer to this question must start from the assumption that
collectively owned enterprises must be at least as publicly accountable
as privately owned ones benefiting from state protection. This means
that, in respect of their broad policy, they will be expected to respond to the democratically expressed demands of the collective
(whether national, regional or local) which owns and controls them.
In so doing, they will take account of a much wider range of
objectives than the narrow accounting targets traditionally associated
with profit-maximizing companies. Such objectives, based on a multi-
faceted perception of what enterprises are for, are likely to include:

- assuring publicly acceptable levels of product quality and diversity;
- meeting specific financial targets, which may or may not include
  a minimum return on capital, but would normally entail ensuring
  the business was self-financing over the medium–long term;
- maintaining given levels of employment within the areas they
  serve, including commitments to stable commercial relations with
  local user and supplier businesses;
- responding to public concerns over the environment or other
  social objectives not directly related to the enterprises' main lines
  of business.

The possibility could also exist of subsidizing enterprises which are
either temporarily insolvent or inherently loss-making, although in
principle this should only be admissible provided certain statutory
criteria were met, including safeguards against unfair competition or
market disruption. Above all it will be vital to abandon the presumption, which has been the besetting flaw of the Keynesian/corporatist
model of capitalism, that public money can be indiscriminately
handed out to enterprises on the assumption that it is bound to have
a positive, 'pump-priming' effect on the wider economy.

In order to make the publicly accountable decision-making process as responsive as possible to community concerns, while also minimizing delays in implementation, it would be desirable to devolve ownership and management responsibility to the local level as much as possible. The pattern of such local collective models of economic organization will tend to vary enormously. However, it should be emphasized that precedents already exist for this kind of structure, such as the Stadtwerke in Germany, which are integrated municipally owned corporations providing power, water and other services to their localities on a self-financing basis (even paying dividends to their citizens from operating surpluses).

AN ELEMENT OF PLANNING

Implementation of the kind of model whose elements are sketched out above would obviously imply the need for significant changes to company law as it exists today in western industrialized countries. Yet legislation alone might not be enough to enable an economy based on cooperation rather than competition to function satisfactorily. This is because in markets which remain totally unplanned, even in the absence of the profit-maximizing dynamic, it would still be open to enterprises and their workforces to seek to expand their level of income by taking markets away from businesses offering the same products or services as themselves. Even if they were to do so without resorting to unfair competitive practices such as predatory pricing, this could prove unacceptably disruptive and contrary to the interests of overall economic efficiency. Hence while under normal circumstances enterprises that failed to meet the demands of consumers would be allowed to close in line with the traditional rules of the market, where the consequence of such closures could be large-scale job losses or the write-off of substantial publicly owned assets, opportunities for salvation would need to be allowed. At the very least, however, there should be a statutory requirement that any decision to subsidize such businesses, even for a short period, should be subject to fully transparent public scrutiny and democratic approval.

Similarly, it would be necessary either to regulate markets to ensure that patterns of trade could not be disrupted through unfair
price or other distortions, or else to provide for some element of
planning of commercial flows. The need for this would be particularly
compelling to the extent that it might be deemed a public interest
(for environmental or other reasons) to encourage the localization of
supply of goods, as, for example, has lately been much discussed in
respect of the livestock industry in the European Union.[3]

Indeed agricultural commodity markets in particular would need
to be subject to mechanisms of control such that prices could be
stabilized at levels that are adequately remunerative to producers without tending to stimulate excess stocks overhanging the market. As
noted earlier, the necessity of intervention in these markets was
accepted in the industrialized world for most of the period since
World War II, only to be briefly scaled back (particularly in the US)
during the liberalization craze of the 1990s. Now that the latter
experiment has demonstrably failed, and resort to some form of
intervention has been found inescapable (see Chapter 4), it seems
certain that renewed control mechanisms will be sought so as to
minimize the cyclical fluctuation of food supplies and prices, at least
in the developed world.

Under the more cooperative model of economic organization
that will be required in future, structured approaches to market
stabilization will be viewed as essential, although they would need to
be far less prone than earlier systems of intervention to stimulating
costly overproduction. At the same time poor countries which
presently cannot afford such market-stabilizing mechanisms, or else
are unable to prevent them collapsing under the weight of corruption and waste, must be assisted to operate them with much
more effective supervision and accountability. Even more importantly
for the Third World, the present distorted and anarchic structure of
world commodity markets must be transformed so as to ensure that
the prices paid by rich countries for commodities which they must
import from tropical countries, such as coffee, rubber and bananas,
reflect the true costs of production. Above all this will mean that the
labour of the primary producers is valued at a level compatible with

basic human dignity, rather than the starvation wages which currently condemn so much of the Third World's rural population to lives which are scarcely an improvement on those of the slaves who worked the colonial plantations in the past.

Such an approach will certainly not be compatible with the existing unstable structure of world commodity markets, which are effectively controlled by or in the interests of the traders and user industries based in the industrialized countries. In future these organizations will no longer be permitted to manipulate markets for their own speculative gain, whether at the expense of producers or final consumers. Likewise development agencies such as the World Bank will no longer be allowed effectively to force poor countries to remain dependent on exports of such commodities, thereby encouraging global overproduction and ensuring a continued real decline in producer prices. Instead production and trade will need to be managed on the basis of a system of quotas and selective intervention designed to ensure stable and equitable prices (for producers and consumers alike) while minimizing the cost to taxpayers. Such mechanisms, which might also include long-term supply contracts between primary producers and importers or processors in consuming countries, will mirror the type of market intervention that will, as suggested above, need to be applied to domestic agricultural sectors once the flaws of liberalized markets start to be recognized again.

MARGINALIZATION OF THE FINANCIAL MARKETS

Insistence that the public interest in the running of privileged and protected corporations must ultimately predominate over that of their private shareholders has another important implication. This is that the power and significance of financial markets in the economy will be greatly diminished compared to what it has been since the mid-nineteenth century. For, as noted above, the propensity of collective, public-sector interests to influence the running of these enterprises in ways which will reduce the returns to shareholders will inevitably tend to depress the prices of their shares and diminish the interest of private investors in holding them. With the passage of time this will obviously mean that fewer and fewer shares will be traded on stock exchanges, especially as an increasing number of bigger corporations come under majority collective ownership by default. Perhaps, indeed, the only shares for which there is likely to be an active market will be those in the more speculative ventures where the absence of limited liability may not be seen as a serious deterrent (e.g. oil or mineral exploration).

One consequence will be that trading in bonds or other fixed interest securities will become relatively more important, but is also likely to offer less scope for profitable investment than in the past. This is mainly because the diminished significance of the business cycle under what should be an inherently more stable economy should tend to reduce the fluctuations in the balance of supply and demand for loanable funds and also in the security rating of companies, thus reducing the volatility of bond values. The degree of security should also be strengthened by the implicit state guarantee associated with enterprises under majority public ownership, in which case the only element of volatility would be that associated with the perceived solvency of the state itself.

At the same time the role of banks and financial institutions in determining the allocation of resources would be much less decisive than it has been, particularly in the recent past. This is because banks, or at least those licensed to take deposits from the public, will need, as now, to be backed by a de facto guarantee of solvency from the state as lender of last resort, but will henceforth for that reason no longer be permitted to pursue goals of competitive profit maximization, nor be tempted into the snare of moral hazard by opportunities for imprudent speculation. Rather they will be required to subordinate their lending and investment strategies to publicly determined priorities, with little scope or incentive for excessive risk taking.

Likewise investor institutions such as mutual funds, units trusts and pension funds would be much diminished in significance compared with their present position. This is obviously because of the greatly reduced interest on the part of the general public in equity investment, whether directly or through institutions, which would prevail under the more restricted regime of corporate accountability and governance described above. Moreover, this waning of investor enthusiasm would be accentuated by the withdrawal of tax incentives to invest for retirement. Indeed, since it is bound to be generally recognized, particularly following the disasters set to befall funded pension schemes during the coming prolonged bear market in equities, that this method of providing pensions is fatally flawed compared with state-run pay-as-you go schemes, pension funds seem certain to disappear almost entirely.

A NEW ECONOMICS

It should be clear from the preceding description of the essential features of a global economic society which could be an alternative to the anarchic one which presently exists that what is needed to make it work is a post-capitalist, post-imperialist ideology. The principles which define it, however, should not amount to some rigid dogma rooted in a narrowly class-based or sectarian formulation of what constitutes freedom or the limits to state power. Nor, by the same token, should it rest on a static and limited perception of the determinants of human behaviour or of any supposedly fixed economic laws of motion (such as 'long waves'). Rather its guiding principles should be based on priorities determined by an ever more democratic expression of popular aspirations in a global environment which will continue to evolve, both socially and physically. From the perspective of the early twenty-first century, such a post-capitalist ideology must encompass certain principles which contrast strongly with those of the currently ruling ideology rooted in the eighteenth-century traditions of bourgeois liberalism and the sanctity of private property. These broad precepts must include the following:

1. *Conscious political choice* This must replace the delusion of consumer sovereignty operating in a marketplace that is at once anarchic and subject to manipulation by sectional, unaccountable vested interests. This does not mean that market forces can in any sense be abolished or ignored, but that visible signals from the market-

place (which may, for example, appear to indicate that there is little demand for this or that product) need to be cross-checked against independent monitoring of public opinion.

2. *A new economic calculus*   This must be developed in place of the crude and simplistic model traditionally applied under capitalism, according to which the only costs and benefits taken account of are those to which the commercial market can ascribe a value. This must be capable of correcting properly the distortions arising under the existing market system from, for example:

- failure to account for 'externalities' (such as the impact of industrial or transport pollution on the environment or public health);
- failure to assign a proper economic value to the role of 'carers' (including those engaged in child rearing or tending disabled relatives), and thus to reflect this in proper compensation through the state welfare system.

3. *A general bias in favour of greater equality of personal income and wealth*   This should be easier to attain to the extent that:

- Profit maximization, competition and risk taking will be severely downgraded as compared with their supposed importance according to traditional capitalist ideology. Hence the justification for paying top managers more in a year than most of their staff could expect to earn in a lifetime will disappear;
- The need is accepted for transfers of funds through the welfare system both to provide economically essential groups such as carers with a proper reward and the socially disadvantaged with a level of income compatible with basic human dignity;
- The need is also accepted for more or less permanent transfers of resources from the wealthier regions of the world to the structurally disadvantaged ones;
- It is perceived that reduced income disparities will make it easier to use indirect taxes to encourage what may be deemed more socially benign forms of behaviour (e.g. charging motorists for driving into city centres) without arousing complaints that this will discriminate against the poor.

CURBING THE POWER OF BIG MONEY

Clearly moves of the kind outlined above to make powerful corporations more accountable to the community on which they depend for protection and subsidy will meet fierce resistance from the privileged interests that are thereby threatened. Yet in the immediate aftermath of the financial and economic crisis which seems set to unfold in the first decade of the twenty-first century it can be expected that these interests will be forced to give ground. In particular this will mean that big business will have to accept:

- reimposition of the relatively tight regulation of financial institutions and markets which existed prior to around 1980 but has since been undone;
- extensive public sector participation in the ownership of major corporations, both industrial and financial, as the price for the state bailing them out of their difficulties during the crisis.

It may be recalled, however, that organized capital has engaged in such tactical retreats in the face of previous crises. Thus in the 1930s the Securities Exchange Act and other laws were introduced in the United States in order to prevent the kind of financial market abuses and instability that had led to the Wall Street crash of 1929, while in the early part of that decade most continental European countries engaged in extensive nationalization of failed banks. Yet 50 years later the removal of most of these restraints has allowed the same banking and financial abuses to reappear in the US and elsewhere, while likewise since 1980 many European public sector banks have been handed back to the private sector.

The ability of private corporate interests thus to submit to increased state control in moments of weakness, only to retake the ground they have given up when conditions permit, is as easy to explain as it is familiar. It is a function above all of the enormous influence, already noted, that big money is able to deploy in influencing the political agenda and the actions of governments. Nowhere has this been more evident than in the pressures brought to bear on the US Congress and the Clinton administration by the banking lobby to secure repeal of the Glass–Steagall Act, thus largely eliminating what remained of US banking regulation, in 1999.[4]

If a repetition of such damaging subversion of political and economic institutions by organized capital is to be avoided in future, it will clearly be necessary to mobilize public opinion in support of a permanent marginalization of corporate influence. It is important to grasp that the opportunity to do this is only likely to arise at a moment in history when: (i) big business has suffered a severe setback in public esteem because of its perceived failure or collective misdemeanours; and (ii) corporate power is weakened by its financial fragility and consequently increased dependence on public largesse. If, as may be anticipated, the presently developing world economic crisis presents such a window of opportunity, it will be vital to take advantage of it so as

1. to move towards a more genuinely participatory democracy than has existed anywhere hitherto, in which no minority sectional interest is in a position to override the wider public interest;
2. to create solid defences against democratic institutions ever being thus subverted again.

The appropriate institutional form of such enhanced democracy cannot be dogmatically determined according to a single blueprint, and should be expected to evolve according to a variety of patterns in a way that reflects different cultural traditions and historical experience. But whatever different models may be adopted, it must be understood that, besides conforming to such basic minimum standards as those laid down in the Universal Declaration of Human Rights, durable democratic constitutions will need to enshrine three types of restrictions against the possibility that the power of money could take control of the system and determine its agenda.

Restrictions on the funding of political parties If the democratic process is to be a genuine expression of the popular will, a minimum condition (though not by itself a sufficient one) is that sectional interest groups not be allowed to gain undue weight in determining its outcome, either by setting the agenda or influencing votes. While this restriction must apply to all such groups – including, for example, trade unions or religious sects – it would obviously be aimed particularly at limiting the influence of business organizations, since money is the main mechanism whereby it is brought to bear. To this end legally constituted political parties will be allowed to receive financial contributions only from individual members, at a single flat rate, to which funding from the state would be added in proportion to the total sum raised from members.

Limit on patronage Public officials, whether elected or appointed, should be barred from accepting:

- any form of emolument (including 'consultancy' fees) other than their official salaries, which should be set at sufficient levels to discourage corruption, while they are in office;
- paid employment with corporations or interest groups of any kind for several years after they leave office, in return for which they would be assured an adequate official pension.

Ownership of the mass media Rules limiting the concentration of ownership would be required, together with guaranteed outlets for minority opinion. Measures to be considered would include the allocation of public funding, to newspapers as well as broadcast media, and related moves to limit the influence of advertisers.

Perhaps no set of rules can be proof against certain determined groups or individuals gaining disproportionate influence. However, some precepts such as those outlined above should make it hard to maintain or re-establish the kind of grotesque pro-business consensus which had overwhelmed the body politic in both America and Britain by the end of the twentieth century, such that even the British Labour Party now proclaims the need to favour the private sector as central to its political strategy.

The transnational dimension

The above description of the kind of more cooperative, non-profit-oriented economic model which needs to replace the present unstable capitalist one has been geared mainly to the assumed needs of a putative single national economy. It will also be apparent that it is more readily applicable to economies which are already developed (such as OECD members). Yet logically, if these principles are valid within national frontiers, then in principle they should be considered applicable in relation to the global economy as well. In practical terms, however, there are some important additional factors to be considered in trying to visualize how they might be applied internationally.

Third World priorities

Whereas in the already developed countries it will be both possible and desirable to manage the economy on the basis of stability (low growth or no growth), this will clearly not be true in respect of poor countries. Indeed, given that they are in any case likely, as was suggested earlier, to be significantly dependent on financial flows from the richer countries, the degree of this dependence will need as far as possible to be reduced rather than increased over time. Hence the economies of poor countries will need to be encouraged to expand so as to enable them to increase their output and national income per head substantially faster than the industrialized countries, which will be expected to grow little or not at all. To make this possible it will be necessary for Third World states to pursue development strategies based as far as possible on increasing their self-sufficiency, preferably in the context of increasing regional economic integration, bearing in mind the limited size of their national markets. For only in this way, by meeting their own huge unsatisfied demand for products and services that have long been accessible to most people in the developed world, will their citizens be enabled to start closing the huge gap in living standards that now separates them from the latter.

Such an approach of course runs totally counter to the prevailing dogma of globalization and the 'Washington consensus', based on rigid adherence to the idea of non-discriminatory free trade embodied in GATT/WTO. However, as noted in Chapter 4, the crumbling of genuine belief in this supposed ideal on the part of most WTO members is reflected in the growing number of bilateral and regional arrangements that have sprung up amongst them. At the same time there is a growing recognition among the countries of Africa, Asia and Latin America of the need to reinforce regional commercial cooperation with monetary integration based on common approaches to macroeconomic policy.[5] Although the neo-imperialist tendency in the US (and to a lesser extent in Europe) may continue to try and thwart such tentative moves towards Third World empowerment, in reality they would hardly threaten the established position of potentially competing producers in the developed countries, the vast bulk of whose existing markets lie outside the Third World.

The necessity of discrimination

Countries which seek to regulate their economies and impose restraints on the private sector in ways such as those outlined above would clearly have an uneasy relationship with those still seeking to uphold the existing economic order based on global free trade. Indeed it is clear that under the present international rules of the game any country attempting to move towards such a model of regulated capitalism would be subject to prosecution and punishment under the rules of the WTO, while any developed country pursuing such an approach might expect also to be expelled from the OECD. Whether or not such sanctions were imposed, however, it would obviously be impossible for any state or group of states adopting a more regulated model to allow unrestricted relations with countries which did not adhere to similar standards. Most obviously, the unrestricted movement of capital across frontiers would be intolerable to the extent that it permitted companies or investors to remove their assets to a more accommodating jurisdiction, resulting in a rundown in the productive capacity of the regulating country and perhaps a damaging run on its currency. Likewise the attempt to impose common minimum standards in respect of employment, the environment and other areas of corporate behaviour affecting competitiveness would preclude open trade relations with countries that were unwilling to accept them. (In this connection it is notable that the decision of the newly formed Bush administration in 2001 to withdraw US support for the Kyoto Protocol on global warming provoked immediate suggestions in some European Union countries that this would make it necessary to consider restrictions on trade with the US.)

Superficially it may seem that insistence on the need for discrimination in international trade, both by Third World countries seeking to enhance their economic self-sufficiency and by developed countries trying to ensure greater domestic stability, amounts to rejection of the principle of globalism enunciated above. However, it should scarcely need pointing out that genuine openness and cooperation among nations requires both (i) an acceptance by different states of minimum common standards of behaviour; and (ii) recognition of the right of seriously disadvantaged nations and communities to receive support from the better endowed, subject to appropriate conditions including the application of genuine democratic accountability. In short, in an international context, replacing competition with cooperation means emphasizing solidarity rather than a Darwinian struggle for survival in which the weakest must expect to perish.

It is self-evident that switching from the present pseudo-*laissez-faire* model of global economy to a more cooperative one presupposes a more open acceptance of the need for official regulation of and intervention in markets. But an equally necessary and still more dramatic change in attitude will be a recognition of the need to move away from the hegemonic model of world political control in favour of one that is based on more genuinely supranational institutions.

CHAPTER 7

THE TRANSITION TO SUPRANATIONALISM

Just as the breakdown of the global economic order based on the capitalist profits system now points the world towards radically new structures in the economic sphere, so the parallel crisis in the neo-imperialist political order calls for a comparably rapid evolution in the organization of international relations. Indeed it is obvious that there is an important interaction between these twin crises which, through its impact on the globally dominant interest groups, makes it impossible to resolve either of them without a fundamental shift in the motivation and priorities driving governments everywhere.

Such a shift, it will by now be evident, must involve downgrading the interests of the tiny élite which presently controls most of the wealth and power in favour of giving primacy to the concerns of the vast majority. Some indication has already been given of the kind of alternative approaches to the structuring and management of the economy (at local, national, regional and global levels) which will be needed to bring order out of the mounting chaos, and which to some extent are already being applied. In the final two chapters an attempt is made to develop a plausible vision of how a more general movement away from the existing order to one based less on the hegemony of big business and the tyranny of the profits system and more on cooperative collectivism might occur.

THE EMPTY SHELL OF SOVEREIGNTY

As noted earlier, the intensifying deterioration in the economic plight of most poor countries, particularly since around 1980, has reduced many of them to a state of effective destitution, with inevitably adverse consequences for international political relations. The associated breakdown of civil order in many parts of the Third World, which has intensified since the end of the Cold War in 1989, has been largely the consequence of this economic failure, although it has also been associated with outbreaks of previously dormant ethnic and religious divisions. The resulting epidemic of 'low-level' conflict in so many countries, often, especially in Africa, spilling across international frontiers, has called in question the durability of the whole post-1945 international political dispensation. In particular, it has increasingly cast doubt on:

- how far most of the world's supposedly sovereign nation states (the majority of which have come into existence since the end of World War II) could ever be expected to attain meaningful economic independence;
- whether states whose boundaries are largely the legacy of European colonialism and subsequent haphazard decolonization after World War II can be regarded as politically sustainable.

The need to confront these issues, which are seldom in fact raised in public debate among the world's leading powers, is bound in turn to raise a question-mark over the central principle of the United Nations Charter, the basic point of reference for the regulation of international relations since 1945. This is the precept that every UN member state's sovereignty is inviolate (Article 2), and that neither any foreign power nor the UN itself may legally intervene in its territory unless invited to do so by the state concerned. The rationale of this principle, designed to deter aggression by countries against one another, may seem superficially to be still largely valid. However, it clearly constitutes a serious obstacle either to dealing with the appalling immediate problems associated with civil breakdown in many states or to effecting any redrawing of boundaries which might be needed to enhance long-term stability.

Indeed with the passage of time this restraint seems rather to serve as an excuse for indifference or denial of responsibility on the part of the Security Council or those countries with the resources to intervene effectively in states where civil authority may have largely collapsed. Refusal to intervene in such circumstances out of supposed respect for national sovereignty seems all the more hypo-critical in so far as the western industrialized nations, and the US in particular, have engaged in systematic subversion of many Third World governments (notably during the Cold War) and continue to coerce them through the conditions attached to development aid and other forms of official blackmail. In short, it is clear that mili-tary invasion is not the only way a country's sovereignty may be compromised.

AMBIVALENCE ON HUMAN RIGHTS

Another glaring anomaly in the way the UN system has developed in practice is the lack of any consistent approach to upholding the principles of democracy, human rights and the rule of law as embod-ied in the Universal Declaration of Human Rights. This document, which was originally adopted unopposed by the UN General Assem-bly in 1948,[1] has subsequently formed the basis for a series of inter-national human rights treaties subject to ratification by member states individually. Yet in spite of the fact that the most important of these treaties, the International Covenant on Civil and Political Rights (CCPR), formally commits the vast majority of UN members who have ratified it to apply its principles[2] since its adoption by the General Assembly in 1966,[3] there has manifestly been continued violation by most signatories of the principles they are pledged to uphold.

The failure of the United Nations to take any action to enforce conformity with its own principles, in clear contravention of the spirit of the rule of law, is obviously a reflection of the interests and attitudes of the key member states, particularly the permanent members of the Security Council. Indeed for most of the UN's history this deviation from its own professed standards has been the inevitable, and widely accepted, consequence of the Cold War rivalry between the western alliance under US leadership and the Soviet bloc. For, as suggested earlier, this struggle was more in the nature of a rather traditional rivalry between two quasi-imperial powers than the contest between competing ideologies that both sides claimed it to be. Hence what counted was to gain the material support of otherwise uncommitted states for either side rather than to win the hearts and minds of their diverse peoples, recognizing that the effective international hegemony of a great power is not compatible with the principles of democracy.

Thus the legacy of the Cold War to the United Nations is a tradition of systematic flouting of the principles of human rights on which the world body was supposed to be founded. It was hardly to be expected that such a tradition would be rapidly overturned once the conflict was over. This is clearly all the more true in that the US, as the sole remaining superpower, will clearly not abandon its quasi-imperialist foreign policy in a hurry just because the principal excuse for maintaining it has disappeared. On the other hand the practical and political difficulties in perpetuating its arbitrary power are considerable.

BEYOND UNILATERALISM

Indeed, for a number of reasons (some of which have already been indicated), the superficially unchallengeable global dominance of the United States in the aftermath of the Cold War is actually far more fragile than might be suggested by its overwhelming military superiority. Such factors, which seem bound to force the US to accept significant compromises, include:

- the deepening economic malaise and associated civil disorder in much of the Third World and the former Soviet bloc countries;
- the impotence of the US military machine in the face of widespread subversion and resistance to its dominance on the part of

large numbers of dissidents around the world who feel they have nothing to lose by taking up arms;

- continuing, and perhaps intensifying, domestic opposition to foreign involvement which may seem politically repugnant or simply irrelevant to perceived US interests, especially if this entails taking significant American casualties;
- growing reluctance on the part of the US's allies to provide material (or even moral) support to policies which may seem to be against their interests or to have little chance of ultimate success;
- the prospect of prolonged financial and economic crisis at home, weakening the US budgetary position and the dollar and thus its capacity to intervene abroad.

It is of course difficult to foresee quite how or over what timescale the US may be forced to make concessions and accept some watering down of its existing unilateralist stance. Yet some indication may perhaps be gained from examining the current approach of the international community, under US leadership, to dealing with some of the numerous crises now confronting it in different parts of the globe.

Military intervention

An obvious symptom of the malaise affecting the world order since the end of the Cold War has been the increasing incidence of outbreaks of low-level conflict in virtually every continent. This has prompted calls for direct intervention by the international community in the internal affairs of UN member states whose governments are either unable to maintain administrative order – if they have not effectively ceased to function altogether – or have engaged in egregious abuses of human rights. The extreme reluctance of the international community to intervene in such states has been repeatedly demonstrated since the start of the 1990s – notably in some notorious cases, such as Bosnia and Rwanda, where their failure to act soon enough resulted in major humanitarian crimes bordering on genocide. Partly as a result of these chastening experiences in the

early 1990s there was a rather greater willingness to act when, at the
end of the decade, the crises in Kosovo and East Timor (respectively
administered by Yugoslavia and Indonesia)[4] forced themselves on
world attention.

Of these two cases the actions of the international community in
Kosovo provide much the most significant indicator both of the
weakness of the existing institutional world order and of the reasons
why there is nevertheless great reluctance to change it, particularly
on the part of the US. This is because the military intervention by
NATO in defence of the Kosovo Albanians, however morally justi-
fiable it may have been, was quite clearly illegal in terms of the UN
Charter. Moreover a UN intervention would also have been illegal
even if it had been approved by the Security Council (rather than
being vetoed by Russia and China), since outside intervention was
opposed by the legally constituted and recognized government of
Yugoslavia.

Notwithstanding this illegality, following the subsequent military
occupation of Kosovo by NATO forces from June 1999 a civilian
administration was constituted in the name of the United Nations
(UNMIK) pending a long-term political settlement in the region.
While such a major and unprecedented deviation from the UN
Charter was extraordinary enough, what stands out is the complete
failure of the UN or its leading members either to attempt any
rationalization of its involvement in Kosovo in terms of general principles or to recognize the need for consequential changes in the UN
Charter. Whatever the precise reasons were for the refusal of the
international community to address this glaring anomaly, there can
be little doubt it was and remains in the perceived interest of the
United States to remain silent over it. This is because any attempt to
address it would have entailed trying to establish generally applicable
criteria for justifying such unsolicited intervention in the territory of
a 'sovereign' state, and therefore, by extension, to define the limits of
national sovereignty.

For it is not hard to see that, were such limits to be established in
codified form, it would be hard for the US or any other power to
resist demands for intervention in any state where the Security

Council might determine that the criteria had been fulfilled. Still more importantly, perhaps, it would make it harder to defend unilateral interventions by the US, such as those in Grenada in 1983 and Panama in 1989. Meanwhile, in the absence of any such clear legal restraint, Washington has resumed (from 1999) what may prove to be a significant degree of military involvement in parts of Latin America under the guise of fighting the 'drugs war'. The most publicized instance of this is the Plan Colombia, although a lower level of US military activity in conjunction with the local armed forces has also now commenced in Guatemala and other Central American countries.[5] In all cases there is a widespread suspicion that the role of the US forces is at least as much one of political counter-insurgency as of anti-narcotics policing, especially in Colombia, where a large part of the national territory is controlled by left-wing rebels.[6] Yet whatever the true motivation behind the US authorities' intervention in these countries, it is obvious they are only too anxious to avoid the creation of any clear rules which might legitimize intervention by the international community in such cases but end the US's ability to take unilateral action.

Judicial intervention

Despite the lack of such a legal framework in relation to Kosovo, which seems destined to become an increasing threat to the legitimacy of UNMIK as a durable settlement of the problem remains elusive, one potentially significant challenge to the inviolability of national sovereignty has already occurred as a result of the appalling tragedies of Bosnia and Rwanda. This is the move to set up a permanent International Criminal Court (ICC), which was initiated when no fewer than 160 UN member states (over 80 per cent of the total) voted to establish it in 1998. The intended remit of this court is to try individuals for the most serious offences of global concern, such as genocide, war crimes and crimes against humanity. Although its stated purpose is to act only in those cases where national jurisdictions are unwilling or unable to indict those suspected of such offences, its clear message is that the international community reserves the right to enforce respect for human rights wherever they may be threatened. The fact that the United States, alone among the developed western nations, has refused to sign it[7] is a sure sign that the US recognizes the ICC as a genuine move to advance the idea of the international rule of law and thus a challenge to its own preferred approach of continued US unilateralism.

Whether or not US opposition to the ICC persists, however, it seems likely that the court will become a reality by 2004, by which date it is projected that the necessary 60 member states will have ratified it and thereby signalled their willingness to submit to its jurisdiction. On the other hand, bearing in mind the failure of most UN member states to honour their commitments to the CCPR and other international codes of conduct they have signed up to, the likely effectiveness of the ICC must clearly be open to doubt.

Economic intervention

It has been noted that for most allegedly sovereign states in the modern world, particularly in the Third World, the economic sphere is where their independence is most obviously and systematically compromised. It is likewise clear that this diminution of their sovereignty stems not only from the legacy of imperialism and the flawed process of decolonization after World War II. It is also a function of the progressively greater involvement of individual sovereign states in each other's economies which has been encouraged and promoted by the international community, particularly the western industrialized nations, ever since 1945. It is this process, culminating in the phase of globalization marking the last two decades of the twentieth century, which has given the US, as the dominant world economic power, the opportunity to exercise very far-reaching intervention in the domestic policies of foreign governments.

In addition to wielding this power to help advance the interests of corporate America in different parts of the world, the United States has increasingly used it to apply pressure on particular states which have proved less than amenable to its broader foreign and economic policies. This is most obviously true of such 'rogue states' as Cuba, Libya, Iran and Iraq, which have displayed open defiance of US hegemony and have consequently been exposed to economic sanctions imposed by the US either unilaterally or, wherever it can gain their support, in conjunction with its allies. Beyond this, however, American power has been deployed – particularly through the medium of the IMF, World Bank and other multilateral development agencies which it largely controls – to try and impose conformity with Washington's neo-liberal ideology, which is of course closely linked to the promotion of its perceived national economic and commercial interests. This is done by means of withholding development aid or financial support in order to compel compliance with US-imposed policies (or conditionality), a form of coercion which clearly amounts to a degree of economic sanctions.

It is striking that, although the UN Charter provides for the authorization of economic sanctions as an appropriate non-military response (which may be mandated by the Security Council) to aggression against a member state, nowhere does it mention the possibility that the application of economic sanctions by one or more states against another without Security Council authorization might itself be deemed an act of aggression. This anomaly thus constitutes an effective loophole in the rules which permits the US, or any member state, to infringe the sovereignty of other countries without any legal restraint, even though other international agreements, such as GATT/WTO, do lay down when such sanctions may or may not be applied. Such is the lack of regard for this point on the part of the US and the rest of the industrialized world that they are quite prepared to set themselves up as global economic policemen to enforce rules which have no legal standing at all, as demonstrated by the attempt of the OECD to impose rules on tax havens (see Chapter 4).[8]

There are growing signs, however, that this type of intervention is creating more problems for the US and the world as a whole than it can ever be expected to solve. This is not simply because such economic coercion tends to create increased hardship for the already impoverished majority in most of the countries that are exposed to it, often while the ruling oligarchies which typically control the government remain largely unscathed, thus intensifying popular disaffection and unrest. Ultimately still more damaging is its impact in undermining the legitimacy of the political process in supposedly sovereign states, even where this takes the form of nominally democratic elections and a degree of freedom of expression is permitted. Hence western propaganda on the need for poor countries to enhance respect for democracy and practise good governance increasingly arouses only cynicism in the Third World and elsewhere.

For the US government the growth of world-wide hostility and resistance to its influence may not in the early years of the twenty-first century seem to pose an immediate threat. Likewise domestic public opinion may remain largely indifferent as long as any collateral damage affecting US interests is confined to occasional atrocities such as the bombing of its embassies or attacks on US military personnel. On the other hand, as noted in Chapter 1, it is difficult for Washington, in the post-Cold War, post-Vietnam era, either to countenance, let alone encourage, the overthrow of elected governments in foreign countries or to commit US ground forces in areas where they could be at risk of serious casualties.

Quite how, when or under what circumstances this American complacency in the face of mounting world disorder might be shattered is clearly impossible to say. However, as the global crisis deepens and unrest inevitably threatens more and more countries, it seems impossible to imagine that the US leadership can contemplate any attempt to retreat into 'fortress America', given its evident determination to resist the rise of any effective supranational authority and the absence of any other combination of powers which might be willing or able to act as an effective or acceptable world policeman. On the other hand it seems quite likely, as demonstrated both by the manifest failure of US policy in the Middle East since 1990 and by the moves to set up the ICC in defiance of American wishes, that the United States will become progressively more isolated in its superpower role. In that event it may well feel compelled, like imperial powers of the past, to expend an ever-increasing share of its resources, human and financial, on attempting to sustain that role.

Alternatively it may conclude that, for all its continued ability to intervene with impunity in the affairs of relatively small, weak states in the Third World, it is not in the broader, long-term interest of the

US to try and pit itself against the rest of the world in defence of the immediate, narrow concerns of particular sections of corporate America. Such may well prove, for example, to be its considered response to the challenge of global warming. This is suggested by the aftermath of the Bush administration's decision in 2001 to reject the international Kyoto protocol on climate change on the ostensible grounds that it would damage US industry and employment. For it is evident that the US government was neither prepared for the ferocity of foreign reaction to this announcement nor in a position to advance alternative proposals for dealing with a problem which many of the administration's supporters denied was an imminent threat to the world.

If, as may be expected, the American public proves little inclined to take up this latter-day equivalent of the White Man's Burden, it is perhaps imaginable that the United States may then be prepared to abandon unilateralism in favour of a multilateral approach to collective security which President Wilson was the first world leader to dream of over 80 years ago. In the meantime the rest of the world will almost certainly feel compelled to make further attempts to move in this direction without the US. Bearing in mind the inevitable uncertainty over how such developments will unfold, it is nevertheless possible to speculate on the most likely form such moves might take.

REFORMING THE UN SYSTEM

The manifest flaws in the design and functioning of the United Nations may be conveniently summarized under two headings:

1. The lack of meaningful independence for the vast majority of nominally sovereign member states;
2. The failure to develop any mechanisms for enforcing adherence to minimum common standards in respect of democracy, the rule of law and respect for human rights.

Bearing in mind the chronic nature of these deficiencies, going back to the onset of the Cold War and the flawed decolonization process in the 1950s and 1960s, it seems hard to envisage any remedy to these weaknesses being achieved solely within the existing UN structures. Given this historic legacy, the vested interests opposed to meaningful change may seem too powerful to make possible any serious moves towards either (i) a genuine sharing of sovereignty within the organization, or (ii) enforcement of common standards as a condition of continued membership.

These obstacles to progress are obviously compounded by the questionable political legitimacy of the UN secretariat itself. Hence, while the flaws referred to above are evidently well understood by its senior officials, the latter are seriously constrained from expressing any criticisms that could cause undue offence to member states, including ones devoid of any democratic legitimacy. Thus it was reported that the resignation of the UN High Commissioner for Human Rights, Mary Robinson, in March 2001 was precipitated by the blocking of funding increases for UNHCR, which in turn was the result of action by Algeria in protest at the High Commissioner's outspoken criticism of its human rights record.[9] Likewise it is well known that the United States has persistently deployed the weapon of withholding its quota of funding contributions to the UN in order to exert pressure on it to favour the US's interests and agenda, thus in effect applying unilateral sanctions against the world body itself. As a result of such pressures the UN has felt constrained to lend public support to the idea of economic globalization, even while pointing out its potential negative consequences for poor communities and countries where the state is too weak to resist the power of 'global companies'.[10]

Such contradictory positions may in fact indicate that the pressures for drastic change in the way the UN operates are about to become irresistible. If this is so it surely reflects mainly the evident recognition within the UN itself that many of its member states do indeed lack the power to exercise sovereignty within their own frontiers. Moreover, in contrast to the neo-liberal rhetoric so fashionable since the 1980s, the UN also insists that effective state authority is an essential condition for assuring both civil peace and economic security.[11] Hence it must also understand that actions to try and fill this power vacuum in many Third World countries are a priority. Yet its ability to undertake this task itself has hitherto been severely limited by the terms of the UN Charter, which ensure that the organization's role is essentially passive and that it can take action in relation to the affairs of any country only if specifically mandated to do so by the Security Council. Moreover, until very recently it has always been understood that any such intervention in a particular country would only be for the purpose of 'peacekeeping' or 'peace-building', the implicit assumption being that the civilian administration would always be in the hands of legally constituted national governments.

However, the crises in Kosovo and East Timor in 1999 clearly called that assumption into question, forcing the Security Council to mandate 'interim' UN administrations in these two territories. Yet this was only done pending the creation of conditions in which a domestic administration could be restored or established. Thus there was no deviation from the principle that all state power is deemed to be vested in sovereign nation states. Nevertheless the possibility clearly exists not only that these UN administrations will have to remain in place for several years, but that the need for similar interventions will arise elsewhere, for example in Somalia or Sierra Leone, where there has been no meaningful civil administration since 1990. In such circumstances two questions seem bound to become increasingly pressing:

1. How will the democratic accountability of a UN-appointed administration be assured?
2. Will it be necessary to find a long-term alternative to the standard model of 'nationhood' for territories where sovereign independence can arguably never be more than a polite fiction (as perhaps in the case of East Timor)?

Any possible answers to these closely related questions would obviously have momentous implications for the future role of the world body and the sustainability of its existing constitution as laid down in the UN Charter. It is perhaps idle to speculate on the circumstances that might lead to a revision of the Charter, although such a process would clearly have to address a whole range of other issues, including the enforcement of adherence to human rights and governance standards. What is perhaps more predictable is that, as noted above, there will be strong resistance to any attempts drastically to alter the status quo, and not only from the US.

In view of this likely constraint to transforming the UN into a more cohesive and accountable international organization with sufficient authority to fulfil the more complex role which today's world demands, it may be more practical to envisage creating a completely new body, much as the UN itself had to be created in place of the discredited League of Nations in 1945. The obvious advantage of such an approach is that it would make it possible to start afresh with a membership which could be self-selecting based on a commitment to upholding minimum standards of conduct (derived from the principles of the Universal Declaration of Human Rights) on a legally binding basis. It may be that the creation of the International Criminal Court could provide a model for setting up such a body, especially if it could demonstrate an effective way of enforcing compliance by members with the rules they had signed up to.

GLOBAL UNITY VERSUS REGIONAL BLOCS

Clearly, as implied above, an important feature of a new or reformed world body would be its legitimacy to assume administrative responsibility, on a basis of democratic accountability to the population affected, for any territory whose government was unable to discharge its functions. However, it seems very doubtful if this body could or should be seen as the prelude to some form of world government in which a single political entity would provide the umbrella authority, on some kind of quasi-federal basis, for a vast number of hitherto sovereign states. This is mainly because a structure of this kind, representing so many and diverse countries, would probably be unable to function as a cohesive whole and might therefore easily end up being more a source of division than of unity.

Rather the role of the new UN would be to promote and facilitate a process of consolidation of small and weak states into regional groupings large enough to constitute substantially self-sufficient economic entities. In order to succeed, this restructuring of the political and economic map of the world would need in large measure to reject the tenets of globalization and non-discriminatory free trade which are central to the present world economic order. Instead it should seek to foster zones of relative economic stability and security which would be insulated from the damaging disruption caused by sudden inflows of surplus goods (subsidized or not) from outside or the even more devastating inflows and outflows of speculative capital of the kind which laid waste so many supposedly emerging markets in the 1990s.

In order to achieve the necessary degree of internal economic cohesion and stability such regional groupings would need to be based on much deeper links than those implied by the creation of a free trade area or customs union. Indeed to assure an adequate level of collective independence they would need to establish and maintain a common currency robust enough to combine domestic price stability with interest rates low enough to permit viable domestic enterprise. Apart from requiring a commitment to limit potentially destabilizing capital inflows and outflows, this would also imply extensive coordination of policy among the governments concerned over issues such as social policy or employment standards, which might otherwise tend to distort competitiveness within the regional grouping concerned. Hence a progressively increasing degree of political integration would also be essential in order to validate effective economic integration.

The idea of such regional economic groupings is of course far from new and has been given some concrete form in the shape of organizations such as the Association of South East Asian Nations (ASEAN),[12] the Mercado Comun del Sur (MERCOSUR)[13] of South America and the Southern Africa Common Market (SACM). However, it is fair to say that these groupings have to date struggled to achieve any progress towards meaningful economic integration in the face of chronic internal differences (political and economic) and indifference, if not outright hostility, on the part of the wider international community. Thus the United States was quick to stamp on a Japanese proposal to create an Asian Monetary Fund in the wake of the East Asian financial crisis of 1997–98.

Although the emphasis should be on maximizing the level of self-sufficiency, this is not to suggest that such regional entities should not engage in trade with each other where this is consistent with optimizing economic efficiency. Such would be the case, for example, where certain commodities were not available locally (such as minerals) or could be imported much more cheaply from other regions with a more appropriate climate (such as natural rubber). Moreover, it should be seen as an important function of a reformed UN system to monitor inter-regional trade relations and to try and ensure, within an appropriate framework of rules, that trade was not used as an instrument of aggression or political victimization by one region against another. Indeed it should be part of the revised role of the World Trade Organization, in a world where bilateral or inter-regional trade agreements are likely to supersede the idea of non-discriminatory free trade, to ensure the full transparency of such deals and adjudicate in disputes.

Another key advantage of the regionalized world economy sketched out above is that it should also facilitate a narrowing of the huge disparities in living standards which continue to disfigure the world. As suggested in the last chapter, one of the features of the model of cooperative collectivism which needs to replace the present one of globalized anarchy is that it would both permit and require the dethroning of maximum growth as a crucial goal of economic policy. Nevertheless it is clearly necessary that Third World countries and regions be enabled to grow much faster than the more developed ones if the gap between them is to be gradually closed. By largely insulating them from unfair and disruptive competition from outside, the protected regional model should permit such a catching-up by the more disadvantaged areas of the world, secure in the knowledge that they will be able to meet their own unsatisfied demand for basic goods and services (including staple foodstuffs) primarily from their own industries.

It is important to stress that any such approach to enhancing global solidarity through regional groupings would need to balance the trend towards greater international and regional integration with an adequate degree of decentralization. This point is all the more vital bearing in mind the need to encourage effective channels of democratic expression and accountability, to be addressed in the next chapter.

THE EUROPEAN UNION:
AN ALTERNATIVE ROUTE TO INTEGRATION

While a reformed United Nations might thus be envisaged as the instrument of a more effective distribution of sovereignty in the global order of the future, the European Union provides a living example of evolution towards regional integration which may well have significant lessons for the rest of the world. It may perhaps be objected that, since the EU's membership has hitherto consisted almost exclusively of rich industrialized countries,[14] it can scarcely be regarded as a role model for the vast majority of poor and disadvantaged countries in the world. Although this is undoubtedly a relevant consideration, the experience of the EU since its inception in 1957 in moving towards an 'ever closer union' while also gradually expanding its membership surely offers some valuable insights into the issues nation states need to confront in seeking to combine their sovereignty.

The link between economics and politics   The EU has always been based on the implicit recognition that durable commercial and economic ties between member states must take account of the particular social, cultural and other concerns of each one and, in general, of the need for social solidarity. Hence, it is understood that gaining the benefits of market integration between countries requires more than just the removal of trade barriers. Consequently, while broadly committed to a belief in the merits of market liberalism, the EU has always retained mechanisms for compensating communities that are disadvantaged by the process of market integration because of their inherent lack of competitiveness. Equally, it is recognized that common institutions must be developed in order to resolve differences consistently with gaining a minimum degree of political acceptance for the necessary harmonization of policies.

The need for representative government   In order to endow joint decisions with an adequate degree of legitimacy, minimum standards of democracy must be established in all member states and applied to the common institutions of the EU. The insistence on adhering to this standard as a condition of membership has perhaps been the union's most impressive achievement to date and has unquestionably been a crucial factor in underpinning the democratization of those member states (such as Greece and Spain) where the recrudescence of militarism has, until quite recently, been a threat.

A common currency   Aside from the absolute necessity of creating a single currency if the single market is ever to be a reality, the establishment of the Euro will be vital to the strengthening of the Union's economic independence and capacity to influence the shape of the new global order.

It is obvious that the EU's relatively vast wealth gives it an enormous advantage in addressing the problems of regional economic integration as compared with the position of less developed regions of the globe. Yet this relative strength (combined with its experience of confronting the problems of integration in Europe) gives it considerable potential as a force for promoting the emergence of effective regional groupings elsewhere in the world. Indeed this is something for which the Union has always expressed support and sought to encourage through its technical assistance programmes, notably in respect of Asia and Latin America.

Arguably, however, the EU might equally provide the basis for another approach to supranational integration going beyond the concept of purely regional groupings. This could take the form of an expansion of the union, outside the European region itself, to include a growing number of relatively poor countries. Indeed it is clear that even among the actual or potential candidates for membership within the existing enlargement process, most of which are ex-communist states from the former Soviet bloc or Yugoslavia, there are some which have living standards barely above Third World levels. Moreover, at least two others, Cyprus and Turkey, are not strictly part of geographic Europe.

It is clear that these countries are attracted to apply for membership largely because of the access it will give them to the huge EU market both for their exports and for their unemployed workers, as well as the benefit they expect to receive in transfer payments from the wealthier parts of the union. In reality it is clear that the absorption of so many relatively poor new members is going to be the biggest challenge facing the EU in the first quarter of the twenty-first century, or indeed in its entire history, and a successful outcome is far from a foregone conclusion. Moreover, such an expansion will be accomplished on a sustainable basis only if there are major changes to the EU's present economic structure. This will clearly involve a drastic reform of the impossibly expensive Common Agricultural Policy, although any change is not likely to be in the direction of fully liberalized markets for farm produce. Indeed, given the likelihood of relatively slow market growth and the danger of continued excess capacity in many sectors of the regional and world economies in the coming decades, the free operation of the European single market will need to be tempered with significant restraints if the goals of stability and solidarity are to be complied with.

Whatever the outcome of this process of dramatic EU enlargement may prove to be, the union's importance as a model to the rest of the world will hinge crucially on its continued insistence on basic standards of democracy, human rights and the rule of law as a condition of membership. Moreover, given the obvious popular demand all over the world for the extension of such standards, it can be expected that the United States will be forced to follow suit if it is not to see its global influence diminish.

It is hard to predict what form or forms of international organization will come to predominate in the post-imperial world which must succeed the age of great power hegemony. What does seem inescapable, however, is that no model can be durable which fails to provide some tangible hope of a more tolerable life for the billions of people who today are systematically marginalized and increasingly without hope. As has already been made clear, any attempt to compensate for the past decades of neglect of this deepening humanitarian tragedy will have to reject the cruel delusions of *laissez-faire* dogma. To ensure that the new order offers a more genuine prospect of meeting popular needs and aspirations, society must provide the means of expressing those aspirations, in as free and undistorted a manner as possible. It will therefore be necessary to develop far more effective democratic structures than have been applied anywhere hitherto and to extend their application to the many countries for which democracy has never before been anything but an empty slogan.

CHAPTER 8

THE PATH TO DEMOCRACY

Although the ideal of democratic government dates back more than two thousand years, the notion that it should be considered a basic human right with universal application has become widely established only in the modern era (from the eighteenth century). Even in this period the theoretical belief that 'all men are created equal' has only been slowly and grudgingly translated into the granting of universal suffrage in those countries, mainly in Europe, North America and Australasia, which have pioneered the establishment of a common citizenship. Hence throughout the nineteenth century and beyond the ruling classes of most of these countries insisted on retaining a property qualification for the franchise. For example, in Britain only a minority of male adults had the right to vote until 1885 and no women were enfranchised until 1918, the date at which universal male suffrage was also finally attained. In a number of continental European countries, moreover, women were not given the vote until after World War II.

Seen from the perspective of human history, therefore, the idea of popular democracy based on mass enfranchisement is still relatively new. Likewise there is a very short collective experience of different voting systems and rules to ensure that the democratic process gives as faithful a reflection as possible of the people's wishes. The least surprising finding to emerge from this experience is that the most influential groups in society have an inherent tendency to try and manipulate the process, by legal or other means, so as to maximize the chances that it will produce outcomes favourable to their inter-

146

ests. All the while, however, the perpetrators of such subversion seek to conceal their intentions behind a smokescreen of eloquent lip-service to the democratic ideal and the sacredness of the popular will.

It is also an understandable legacy of past efforts to restrict extension of the franchise that money has remained a powerful influence in determining both the content of the political agenda (the range of key issues to be addressed) and the balance of voter support for particular parties and candidates. This influence is exercised not only through the direct financing of political parties but also via the control of the mass media and other opinion-forming organizations such as book publishers and educational institutions. It has persisted in spite of a long-standing recognition that such bias can lead to a distortion of the democratic process and the enactment of successive measures in many countries to try and restrict it. The failure to ensure that such measures are effective (whether because of·inadequate drafting of rules or weak enforcement) may be ascribed to:

- the ease with which politicians and parties that have a reasonable prospect of attaining office typically succumb to the corrupting power of money;
- the effective natural conspiracy among those who control opinion-forming organs to stifle any discussion of possible restrictions which might undermine the corrupt system which is so vital to perpetuating their power.

Another factor which may explain the chronic collective unwillingness to address this major flaw in the institutions of the world's self-styled democracies is the absence of any mention of the issue in the Universal Declaration of Human Rights or in any other basic international documents on human and political rights.

A CRISIS OF CREDIBILITY

Yet while even in the world's supposedly most advanced democracies the influence of the moneyed interest in politics has never been adequately checked, in the late twentieth century its power to subvert the democratic process ran out of control to an extent not seen since universal suffrage was established. Arguably indeed this tendency has become so pervasive as effectively to overturn many of the political reforms which outlawed previous abuses, such as those in Britain which until 1832 permitted the open buying of votes in the absence of secret ballots. This has been achieved by means of financial contributions from private sector corporations to the funds of political parties such as to ensure that their electoral platforms correspond quite closely with the agenda of big business. Moreover, to the extent that such pressure has been applied to all major political parties, most conspicuously over the years in the United States but also latterly in Britain and other European countries as well, it has had the effect of reducing these supposedly pluralist democracies to the condition of de facto one-party states.

In the US this tendency has become so well established that, in the absence of any meaningful restraints on corporate contributions to political parties, national elections now take the form of a Dutch auction in which the major parties compete for the favours of big business by offering them ever greater concessions, inevitably at the expense of the public interest. The appearance of a similar phenomenon in Britain has been identifiable at least since the 1997 general election, as the Labour government has pursued a neo-liberal agenda virtually indistinguishable from that of the previous Tory administration, even though the latter had just been so emphatically rejected by the voters. Likewise the US (often through the agency of the IMF) routinely forces elected governments in the Third World to abandon election commitments which are not congenial to Washington, while at the same time insisting that any attempts to overthrow the 'democratic' regime will provoke a severe US response.

In developed countries the reaction of public opinion to this high-level subversion has to date been quite muted and passive, to the extent that most people have been able to discern what is going on through the media obfuscation. In the US, where the phenomenon has perhaps been most conspicuous, growing cynicism has been reflected in a steady decline in the level of voter participation in presidential elections (from 64 per cent in 1960 to barely 50 per cent in 2000) while that in congressional elections has shrunk to little more than one-third in years when there is no presidential election. Signs of similar apathy were dramatically demonstrated in Britain by the turn-out of only 59 per cent of the electorate in the 2001 British general election – the lowest level since universal suffrage was instituted in 1928.

What the ultimate effects of this blatant buying of the democratic process will be is hard to assess. In the US the need for party finance reform was for the first time given prominence in the 2000 presidential election, when Ralph Nader (running as Green Party candidate) was able to win 3 million votes by highlighting this issue – despite an effective media boycott of his campaign.[1] Yet arguably it is only likely to become a major focus of political struggle as and when the neo-liberal agenda that is presently the focus of enforced unanimity among the mainstream parties is perceived to be clearly in conflict with the material interests of a majority of the public. In such circumstances any sustained attempts to frustrate expression of the popular will may provoke growing resort to direct action and other forms of extra-constitutional resistance to nominally democratic governments. Equally, on the other hand, it is conceivable that the ruling establishment is quite prepared for such a response and may hope to use it as an excuse for drastic measures such as assuming emergency powers and the suspension of civil rights.

THIRD WORLD CONTRADICTIONS

In the developing world, where political and other forms of corruption are more obvious and the conditions of life for the masses are far less tolerable than in the US or Britain, the response to such abuses is often more explosive. This has been demonstrated by popular uprisings against legally elected governments in numerous states from the late 1990s (notably Ecuador, Côte d'Ivoire and Pakistan). While the motivation behind such revolts may differ in detail, they all signify a widespread belief that the elected government has betrayed its mandate and lost any claim to be representative of the popular will. Such perceptions are inevitably reinforced by conspicuous instances of external intervention (whether by the IMF or other unaccountable foreign interests) to force the government to change its policy. Indeed the almost total absence of any restraints or transparency requirements relating to sources of party funds, whether from local or foreign interests, helps to ensure that the electoral process is even more corrupt than in industrialized countries. Hence despite the fact that since the mid-1980s Latin America has nominally purged itself of military dictatorships in favour of democratic regimes, the legitimacy of most governments in the region is increasingly being called in question.[2]

This problem naturally poses a particular dilemma for the United States. For while on the one hand it has remained, either directly or though the agency of the IMF and World Bank, the world's principal subverter of Third World governments' sovereignty, it has been obliged (particularly since the Cold War) to assume the role of principal defender of Third World democracy. Moreover, its ideological position has been further contorted by the support of successive US administrations for the concept of the 'minimalist state' and the view that governments are more of a hindrance than a help to economic development. Yet, as evidence has mounted of the dangers arising from the increasing fragility of the state in many developing countries, by the late 1990s the US felt constrained to backtrack from this position, as indicated by an increasing flow of policy documents from organizations such as the World Bank emphasizing the vital role of the state and the importance of 'good governance'.[3]

Yet a very important lesson to emerge from the experiments of developing countries with democracy and the debate over governance is that no system of government will gain acceptance unless it proves able to deliver, or can be compatible with, a satisfactory material outcome for most of the population. This does not mean, as many paternalistic rulers of developing countries are prone to suggest (much as their erstwhile colonial masters used to do before independence),[4] that most people in the Third World are too poor and ignorant to care about democracy and human rights. What it does suggest is that material security and democratic government are mutually reinforcing phenomena, and that the continuation of mass poverty (especially where there are huge disparities of wealth within a given society) is bound to be taken as demonstrating that no government that presides over it can be a genuine democracy. In fact the extensive disillusionment with electoral processes which are simply a figleaf for continued unrepresentative government may be linked to an emerging tendency among aid agencies to stress the need for 'participation' and 'empowerment' of poor people at local level as crucial to development.

Despite all these contradictory tendencies, it would seem unlikely that a sustained reversion to authoritarianism in either the developed or the developing world could be politically acceptable either to the United States or the rest of the world community, however much certain diehard elements might hanker after it. Rather, it seems clear that the time has now come for a further advance towards more genuinely representative democracy if global political and economic stability are to be assured for the future. Given the dominant role that the private corporate sector has come to assume under latter-day capitalism, it will be essential for any process of democratic reform to encompass a drastic revision of the rights and functions of corporations as well as the institutions of state which are normally understood to constitute the body politic.

THE NEED FOR ECONOMIC DEMOCRACY

Indeed, as the history of the late twentieth century has revealed, the crucial relationship driving and sustaining the global power structure has increasingly become that which links: (i) the huge and un-accountable power of big corporations; (ii) their growing dependence on state support for survival; and (iii) their ability to buy the political process. Yet, as suggested in earlier chapters, the insatiable demand of the corporate sector for a greater share of resources, most graphically demonstrated by its attempt to place ever more public services in the grip of the private profit system, has subjected the rest of the community to increasingly intolerable pressures. Hence this process of intensifying corporate domination has reached the point where there is now a widespread perception that the advancing tide must not only be halted but reversed. Indeed such is the evident strength of pressure for action in this area that even many would-be defenders of the corporate sector have been forced to propose remedial measures.

As noted earlier, however, the formulae most favoured by the establishment for addressing this problem, such as involving 'stakeholders' or 'civil society' in their decision taking,[5] can never amount to more than the most empty of gestures. In short, their approach amounts to a public relations exercise designed to suggest that something is being done to meet public concerns over excessive corporate power, even as it becomes clearer by the day that no serious action can be taken to control it without demolishing the whole house of cards.

Yet it is a clear conclusion of the present analysis that a breaking point in this fragile relationship cannot be averted for much longer. The only uncertainty is whether breakdown will occur because of an uncontainable popular backlash against the further subordination of the public interest to that of private corporations or (more probably) due to a systemic financial collapse so severe that governments will be unable to mobilize the resources to offset it. At the time of writing it seems plausible to suppose that these two forms of pressure may converge to cause a simultaneous and terminal defeat for big business on both fronts. This is suggested by the humiliating climbdown of the supremely profitable global pharmaceutical industry in its attempt to prevent the South African government from producing cheap anti-HIV drugs in defiance of corporate 'intellectual property rights', at a time when world stock markets were apparently approaching catastrophic meltdown. Whenever and however such a setback happens, however, it seems hard to believe that corporate power will not soon find itself permanently restrained from ever again inflicting such damage on the rest of society.

Yet the overthrow of the tyranny of big business will take longer and perhaps be less enduring to the extent that more acceptable and effective alternative models for managing society are not developed and implemented. In formulating any such alternative it will be vital to recognize that the economic dimension of social and political relationships is of crucial importance. This is because the central issues of political debate nearly all ultimately turn on choices about the allocation of economic resources. It follows that the way in which such resources are generated and distributed, and the mechanisms for deciding this at every level, are matters of just as much concern to the public as the way in which governments are elected and held to account. It is therefore necessary to consider the principles on which enterprises and other institutions of key economic significance will be run in a post-capitalist society, recognizing that no individual organization will be able to determine its actions in isolation from the rest of the economy.

CORPORATE GOVERNANCE IN THE NEW ORDER

As pointed out in Chapter 6, the first principle to be applied to the regulation of corporations in a more sustainable economic order is that they must be subject to effective public accountability wherever they benefit from privileges or special protection conferred by the state. Economists and other analysts from the time of Adam Smith onwards have rightly worried over the problem of how in the real world corporations can be made as accountable to their shareholders as they are supposed to be in legal theory – or, in other words, how to prevent the effective separation of control from ownership. Henceforth, however, this question will seem of lesser importance than that of how to ensure that any organization benefiting from state support, be it under private or public ownership, is made properly accountable to the community for its actions.

If, as we have suggested, private enterprises that enjoy such public support, including the privileged protection of limited liability, are subject to tight constraints on their freedom to maximize profits, an increasing proportion of them are likely to fall under predominantly state ownership as their private shareholders get discouraged. The mere fact of collective ownership (of whatever kind) will obviously be no guarantee that businesses will deliver the performance and benefits to the public that will ultimately be the sole justification for their continued existence. Hence it will clearly be necessary to set criteria by which the public can judge their usefulness in serving the public good. Such criteria, which would be enshrined in company law and subject to transparent procedures of monitoring and enforcement, are indicated in Box 8.1.

The success of this kind of approach will obviously depend on: (i) total transparency in the way businesses are managed; and (ii) effective public representation on the concerned boards of directors. It is also evident that such a model of governance is far more likely to work satisfactorily where the enterprise concerned serves a largely local market. In contrast it would clearly be much more difficult for it to function effectively in the case of a transnational company with operations in different continents but with its ultimate decision-making authority located centrally in Detroit or Tokyo. However, given that the basic requirements of public accountability as outlined earlier would tend to make the continuation of such corporate empires at best much less attractive, and ultimately quite unsustainable, it may be expected that there would in any case be a shift over time to more locally oriented enterprises.

It should be obvious that such an approach to corporate governance could also be applied to public sector organizations which are not in any sense commercial enterprises but which provide services to the general public. Although such bodies (including public health and education services) are of course already publicly accountable in a formal sense, mechanisms need to be developed to make them more responsive to local concerns within the inevitable financial restraints they must be subject to.

INTEGRATION AND INCLUSION

While both enterprises and public service bodies should be enabled to operate with a significant degree of local autonomy, subject to appropriate accountability, they would also be required to take account of linkages within the wider economy in determining such

---

Box 8.1 *Corporate governance: agenda for the future*

Aims and objectives To supply goods and services which are in line with public demand in terms of quality, quantity and price and to respond to changes in demand. Where appropriate the requirement for companies to innovate would entail their collaboration with publicly funded research institutes. (Thus, for example, pharmaceutical corporations would not only be subjected to controls over the setting of prices for drugs of vital importance to disadvantaged groups; their research and investment programmes would be heavily influenced by publicly determined priorities as to which diseases were of greatest importance to be combated.)

Responsibility to the wider economy Firms must respond to public concerns and priorities in respect of levels of employment and support for the local economy (e.g. by maintaining linkages to their suppliers, subject to the latter's adequate performance).

Social obligations Adherence to optimum standards in respect of employment rights, health and safety at work and environmental protection.

Quantitative measures of performance While in general rigid adherence to a minimum rate of return on capital employed would not necessarily be sought, it would normally be assumed that any enterprise would need to cover its costs (including necessary capital replacement) from revenues in order to justify its continued existence.

---

matters as the level of prices and salaries. Indeed mechanisms would need to be developed to determine the pattern of income distribution, including the levels of taxation and transfer payments as between organizations which directly generate revenues and those which do not.

For in an economy where competition and profit-maximization were largely absent, income determination could no more be left to supposedly impartial market forces than could other decisions on resource allocation, such as investment priorities. Indeed such conditions would make it both possible and necessary to decide such matters, as well as those relating to the length of the working week and the appropriate age of retirement, free of the tyranny of the profits system. The only limits would be those imposed by the overall size of the economic resources (allowing for appropriate redistribution as between local, national and regional entities).

Within this framework of an economy treated as an integrated whole, it would also be possible to give proper recognition to those contributions to it that could never be taken account of under capitalism. Most notably, this could include assuring the independent right of those engaged in full-time child-rearing, or other 'carers', to receive an adequate income from the state, rather than treating them as outside the working population.

Above all, as noted in Chapter 6, the essence of a post-capitalist economy would be the substitution of conscious political choice for the dictates of blindly destructive or dishonestly manipulated market forces. That is not to say that market forces could be ignored, let alone abolished; indeed to a great extent they would continue to determine the pattern of supply of goods and services. However, even on the reasonable assumption that market forces could be largely purged of the distortions and misinformation that too often affect them under the profits system, they could not be expected to be the basis of all economic decisions.

The making of deliberate political choices based on considerations going beyond market forces – such as deciding to raise extra taxes or charges from public services in order to cross-subsidize an activity that might not necessarily cover its costs – is hardly likely to be a problem-free procedure. If it is to work, moreover, complete transparency and access to information must be assured. To this end democratic institutions and procedures must be devised which maximize the scope for popular participation but minimize the risk of manipulation.

MAKING GOVERNMENT MORE REPRESENTATIVE AND ACCOUNTABLE

It is scarcely possible, or indeed useful, to try and speculate on the precise institutional forms that democracies will assume in a world where primacy will be given to genuinely reflecting the wishes of voters rather than simply manipulating them. It is important, however, to set some general principles which must be the basis of any truly representative system.

Restricting the influence of moneyed interests Preventing those with disproportionate wealth from gaining undue influence over the agenda of political parties and over the opinions of voters is the single most important area of reform needed to enhance the quality of democracy, both in those western societies where representative government is already well established and elsewhere. The only effective way of achieving such reform will be to outlaw any contributions to parties' funds other than the flat-rate subscriptions of members. To compensate for the loss of funding needed for campaigns, parties with a defined minimum number of members would be entitled to claim funding from the state in a fixed proportion of the audited subscriptions raised from members. Comparable restraints would need to be devised on organizations set up to campaign in referenda or in support of single issues.

Access to the media for divergent opinions The ability of individuals or sectional interest groups to gain effective editorial control over significant parts of the media would need to be sharply curtailed. The scope for individual media magnates to exercise the kind of dominance over major newspapers or broadcast media channels that is now commonplace in most of the industrialized world could be eliminated by withdrawing their right to limited liability status, except on condition that they accepted some form of effective guarantee of balance in both reporting and comment. The need for other forms of regulation would need to be reviewed in the light of changes in the technology and economics of the media, such as may facilitate much easier and cheaper access by minority groups through channels such as the Internet.

Empowering the voters Even if democratic institutions can be purged of the distorting power of money and unfairly biased media, it will still be necessary to restructure them in such a way as to give a more effective voice to the mass of voters. To do this will require abandoning the idea that the holding of elections to choose a government every 4 to 5 years represents an adequate expression of the popular will. This is all the more true where the main parties contesting the election present manifestoes which are often drafted without even submitting them to proper consultation with party members, let alone broader sections of the public. Furthermore, since parties (unlike commercial advertisers) can routinely break any pledges they make without risking any legal penalty, the power of the voters is limited to that of inflicting periodic electoral defeat on whichever party is in power. To overcome these limitations of the conventional electoral process far greater resort to referenda will be called for in future so as to ensure adequate consultation of the public before major legislative changes are enacted. Moreover, to avoid the voters remaining in a purely passive role, mechanisms must be devised to enable fringe parties and campaigning groups to draft constitutional amendments and other legislation and submit them to popular ballot. Furthermore, with the advent of modern communications technology it should be possible to use this type of consultation over non-legislative decisions, particularly at local level.

Limiting patronage One of the most corrupting features of contemporary western democracy is the enormous power of patronage typically placed in the hands of high officials. In particular the head of the executive branch (as president or prime minister) is generally accorded sole discretion over the hiring and firing of members of the cabinet and other senior officials. This type of arrangement, of which Britain is one of the most blatant exponents, obviously gives great coercive power to the leader and inevitably tends to make a mockery of the idea of collective cabinet government, not to mention that of the supreme authority of parliament, most of whose members are solely motivated by seeking preferment through pleasing their party leaders. The only way to rid the system of this in-built distortion will be to strip the chief executive of the power to make such appointments by conferring it instead on the legislature – or a committee appointed by the latter. This should be seen as part of a broader effort to encourage those politicians who are motivated by public service rather than by personal ambition or acquisitiveness. In other words, the ethos would emphasize that holding public office was a duty rather than a privilege.

Holding officials to account In addition to reform of the way public servants are elected or appointed, efforts to make democratic systems more representative and accountable would also need to focus on holding officials to account once appointed. This would involve measures to ensure both that commitments and obligations were adhered to, and that no conflict of interest or opportunity for personal gain had been introduced or sought. This would mean requiring officials and their departments:

- to submit to regular scrutiny of their performance by elected representatives of the public, who should have power to censure the officials concerned or even remove them from office;
- to abstain from any other gainful employment or receipt of gifts while in office and to decline any offers of employment after leaving office with bodies affected by his or her decisions or actions while still in office.

A crucial feature of any system seeking to guarantee genuine accountability would be absolute transparency and public access to all information and documents relating to government activities, except in certain very limited and clearly defined areas. The US Freedom of Information Act should be looked on as the appropriate starting point for any legislation in this connection.

It goes without saying that powerful groups with a vested interest in the status quo will fiercely resist any significant change in the direction outlined above, and indeed will use their prominent combined voice in the media to dismiss proposals for such reforms as utopian and impractical. Yet such arguments may carry limited weight at the end of a period when it has not only proved possible for a tiny minority of the wealthy to subvert and debauch what are claimed to be the world's most advanced democratic systems, but when their ability to do so has manifestly resulted in such huge economic and social damage. Moreover, if this massive perversion of the system has demonstrated, as suggested above, that western democratic institutions are too weak to prevent a recurrence of the kind of corruption that was rife in the British political system before the reforms of the nineteenth century, it follows that:

- either radical reform and strengthening of the system is needed;
- or democracy is an unattainable dream which might as well be abandoned in favour of some form of benign autocracy (in line with the precepts of the seventeenth-century philosopher Thomas Hobbes).

Confronted with such a choice, it may seem unlikely that many societies in the west will readily opt for the second alternative, particularly in the light of Europe's experience of rejecting democracy in favour of fascism in the 1920s and 1930s. It likewise seems scarcely credible that the more authoritarian types of regime which have been traditional in most other parts of the world will remain acceptable to their people, who are now both more aware of alternatives than in the past and less tolerant of political systems which have delivered even less satisfactory material outcomes than have occurred in the west.

It is vital to understand, however, that institutional change alone will not suffice to bring about the more rational and stable form of society that so many crave. Rather there must be a widespread absorption and conscious acceptance of certain guiding principles as the essential basis of economic and social organization. Two in particular stand out as crucial to the durability of the kind of global order based on deepening democracy which has been sketched out in these last chapters and which we may dare to hope might emerge from the present ruinous anarchy:

1. *The idea of equity*, which is clearly implicit in the notion of equality before the law enshrined in the Universal Declaration of Human Rights.

2. *The principle of solidarity*, which lies at the very root of the creation of the United Nations.

It will be clear to many that the spirit behind these fundamental principles has been largely absent from the conduct of human relations in the last two decades of the twentieth century, at a time when the dominant ideology has been one of neo-liberal individualism. If the latter had proved compatible with halting the global spread of economic chaos and associated social and political breakdown, which began with the collapse of the post-war boom in the early 1970s, most people might have been willing to overlook its deficiencies in regard to respect for such principles. In the event its inability to prevent still greater economic and social catastrophe by the dawn of the new century must surely signify that it has failed the ultimate test.

It is hard to believe that future historians will not come to view the present reactionary phase of world politics as a desperate but cynical attempt to save a failed and increasingly dysfunctional profits system from the final overthrow which might have seemed its inevitable fate after the collapse of the Keynesian variant in the 1970s. Yet if to this end the basic values of equity and solidarity which the UN system was intended to uphold have been set aside for a generation, there are surely grounds for hoping that the experience may have taught the world two salutary lessons: (i) the intolerable consequences of attempting to revive and perpetuate outmoded economic and political systems such as *laissez-faire* capitalism and imperialism; and (ii) that the recurrence of genocide and similar crimes against humanity will be avoided only if democracy and the rule of law are established on more solid foundations.

NOTES

INTRODUCTION

1. Soon to be followed by those in Brazil, Turkey and Argentina
2. George Soros, *The Crisis of Global Capitalism*, London, Macmillan, 1998; Warren Buffett, Address to Annual Meeting of Berkshire Hathaway Inc., May 2000
3. A more detailed exposition of the reasons for regarding an epoch-making world financial and economic crisis as a certain prospect are set out in the author's earlier work *The Trouble with Capitalism: An enquiry into the causes of global economic failure*, London, Zed Books, 1998.

CHAPTER 1

1. E.J. Hobsbawm, *The Age of Revolution 1789–1848*, London, Abacus, 1977.
2. In August 1941, before the US had actually entered the war.
3. Other than the white dominions such as Canada.
4. George Kennan, State Department document PPS 23, February 1948, cited in N. Chomsky, 'Intervention in Vietnam and Central America: Parallels and differences', in J. Peck, ed., *The Chomsky Reader*, London, Serpent's Tail, 1988.
5. Indeed US belief in its 'manifest destiny' to dominate the entire American hemisphere had long jarred with its claims to moral superiority over the established colonial powers of Europe.
6. To use the phrase coined by President Eisenhower when he warned (at the end of his term of office in 1960) of the excessive influence of the comparable pressure group in the US.
7. Notably in respect of the possible reunification of Germany – see N. Chomsky, *World Orders, Old and New*, London, Pluto Press, 1997
8. By mining the port of Corinto in 1982.
9. It would doubtless also seem particularly bizarre coming just a few

years after Pope John Paul II was moved to apologize for the original Crusades against Islam launched by the Church 900 years ago.

10. The impetus for the creation of such a court arose from the upsurge in mass atrocities in the 1990s and the perceived need to avoid having to set up ad hoc tribunals to deal with each specific outbreak, as in the cases of the Former Yugoslavia and Rwanda.

11. Definitions of terrorism and aggression have yet to be agreed among the states party to the statute.

12. Cf. Arnold Toynbee, *A Study of History*, Oxford, Oxford University Press 1948; Paul Kennedy, *The Rise and Fall of the Great Powers: Economic change and military conflict 1500–2000*, London, Unwin Hyman, 1988.

CHAPTER 2

1. International Monetary Fund, *World Economic Outlook*, September 1999, Chapter 1.

2. To use the phrase coined by a leading pro-capitalist economist of the twentieth century, who nevertheless acknowledged the validity of Marxist analysis in this respect. See J.A. Schumpeter, *Capitalism, Socialism and Democracy*, London, George Allen & Unwin, 1943.

3. Organization for Economic Cooperation and Development. Until 1994 this body comprised only the 'western' industrialized nations of North America, western Europe, Japan and Australasia, although subsequently the Czech Republic, Hungary, Mexico, Poland and South Korea have been admitted to membership.

4. As noted by Lord Beveridge in his 1942 report which was the guiding document of the post-war British welfare state.

5. If there was ever any doubt that the real purpose of privatization in Britain was private corporate rather than public gain, it has been definitively dispelled by the huge cost to the public purse of rail privatization both before and since its implementation in 1996, not to mention the officially recorded decline in the quality of service.

6. Affecting especially the US, Japan and Scandinavia.

7. See P. Mullan, *The Imaginary Time Bomb*, London, I.B. Tauris, 2000.

8. Still more extraordinary was the conversion of Mr Greenspan to being an enthusiastic proponent of this idea following his early scepticism, which even caused him to suggest in October 1996 that stocks were overvalued – at levels which were little more than half those he was happy to justify four years later.

9. Cf. John W. Hunt, 'Accountants fail to get the measure of the person', *Financial Times*, 30 August 2000.

10. See H. Shutt, *The Trouble with Capitalism: An enquiry into the causes of global economic failure*, London, Zed Books, 1998.

11. Cf. P. Hawken, A.B. and L.H. Lovins, *Natural Capitalism: The next*

industrial revolution, London, Earthscan, 1999.

12. Cf. J.A. Hobson, *Imperialism*, London, James Nisbet, 1902.

13. Even though a few East Asian countries (including China) for a time achieved spectacular growth rates in the 1980s and 1990s.

14. Cf. Ha-Joon Chang, 'The Political Economy of Industrial Policy in Korea', *Cambridge Journal of Economics*, 17, 1993, pp. 131–57.

15. Not only by the increasing prevalence of political corruption but most conspicuously by the high-profile distortion of the voting process in the 2000 US presidential election.

16. This risk is already manifest in the example of China, which is making a clearly more successful (if hardly problem-free) transition to a market economy despite (or perhaps because of) maintaining quite rigid controls on financial and trade flows – a fact noted by none other than the World Bank's chief economist (see J. Stiglitz, *Whither Reform? Ten years of the transition*, World Bank, April 1999).

17. The reality of company boards whose members are free to vote themselves and each other huge awards, even in the face of failing performance, without meaningful restraint from shareholders has come increasingly to public attention since the 1980s. See R. Monks and N. Minow, *Corporate Governance*, Oxford, Blackwell, 1996.

18. See Richard Lapper and Edward Luce, 'Extreme to Mainstream', *Financial Times*, 9 June 1997; H. Shutt, *The Trouble with Capitalism*, pp. 120–24.

19. This tendency, which has extended to other former Soviet republics, has even involved western banks and aid agencies (perhaps even including the IMF itself) in conniving at illicit capital flight and manipulation of exchange and interest rates to the benefit of small numbers of favoured speculators – with ruinous consequences for the already impoverished economies concerned. See S. Pirani and E. Farrell, 'Western financial institutions and Russian capitalism', paper delivered at academic conference on The World Crisis of Capitalism and the Post-Soviet States, held in Moscow on 30 October–1 November 1999.

CHAPTER 3

1. Charles Wilson, President of General Motors, to a congressional hearing on his appointment as Secretary of Defense, 1953.

2. While this is arguably less true in respect of telecommunications since the advent of wireless telephony – avoiding dependence on land lines – it is still the case that the fixed investment involved in creating a mobile telephone network is substantial, while in any case the finite availability of band-width means that operators must be licensed and therefore constitute at least a 'natural oligopoly'. Equally, because of the industry's role as an essential public service (providing emergency call facilities) operators must in any case be regulated.

3. Michael Heseltine, Secretary of State for Defence under the Thatcher administration 1983–85.

4. First noted by the classical economist T.R. Malthus (1766–1834).

5. As famously recorded by Friedrich Engels in *The Condition of the Working Class in England* (1845), Oxford, Blackwell, 1971.

6. J.K. Galbraith, *The Affluent Society*, London, Hamish Hamilton, 1958.

7. In the words of Stanley Baldwin, British Conservative prime minister of the inter-war period.

8. Cf. *Employment Policy*. Cmnd 6527, London, HMSO, 1944; *Action Against Unemployment*, Geneva, ILO, 1950.

9. Other than by a few *laissez-faire* fundamentalists such as the Austrian economist F.A. von Hayek

10. Perhaps because of their more recent history of feudalism.

11. See E. Swyngedouw, F. Moulaert and A. Rodriguez, 'Large-scale urban development projects: A challenge to urban policy in European cities', in *Urban Redevelopment and Social Polarisation in the City*, European Union (DG XII) 1999; Joan Ely Fitzgerald and Kevin R. Cox, 'Urban Economic Development Strategies in the USA', *Local Economy*, February 1990 (LEPU, South Bank Polytechnic, London).

12. This repealed the Glass–Steagall Act of 1933, enacted to curb the banking excesses which helped to cause the crash of 1929, without doing anything to reduce the moral hazard problem. See 'Triumph of the suits', in *FOMC Alert*, 21 December 1999, Financial Markets Center, Philomont, VA.

13. Marshall Auerback, 'When will the US play the final moral hazard card?', www.prudentbear.com, 13 October 2000.

14. Lanny Baker, managing director of Salomon Smith Barney, quoted in *Financial Times*, 10 January 2001.

15. Cf. 'Renewing the covenant with investors', speech by SEC Chairman Arthur Levitt to the New York University Center for Law and Business, 10 May 2000.

16. Inaugural address, March 1933.

17. 'US may ease stance over money laundering', *Financial Times*, 1 June 2001.

18. H. Shutt, *The Trouble with Capitalism: An enquiry into the causes of global economic failure*, London, Zed Books, 1998, Chapter 14.

19. To a large extent they are not even accountable to their shareholders, while in many cases power is effectively concentrated in the hands of the chief executive, who often has little difficulty in manipulating other board members; see R. Monks and N. Minow, *Corporate Governance*, Oxford, Blackwell, 1996.

20. W. Hutton, *The State We're In*, Jonathan Cape, London, 1995.

21. *Daily Express*, 16 January 2001.

22. A combination of stagnating economic growth and high inflation, as was experienced in the mid-1970s.

CHAPTER 4

1. *Principles of Political Economy and Taxation*, 1817, Chapter VII.
2. Joan Robinson, *The New Mercantilism*, inaugural lecture at Cambridge University, Cambridge, Cambridge University Press, 1966.
3. Estimates derived from Eurostat 1999 Labour Force Survey report.
4. Richard Layard, 'Clues to prosperity', *Financial Times*, 17 February 1997.
5. Addressing the Labour Party Conference 1999.
6. Even after allowing for the substantial proportion of total economic activity in these countries that takes place outside the formal economy, or even the cash economy.
7. H. Shutt, *The Myth of Free Trade: Patterns of protectionism since 1945*, Oxford and London, Basil Blackwell and The Economist, 1985.
8. W.M. Scammel, *The International Economy since 1945*, London, Macmillan, 1980.
9. John A. Hobson, *Imperialism*, London, Allen & Unwin, 1948.
10. Deepak Lal, *The Poverty of Development Economics*, Institute of Economic Affairs, London, 1983. Amazingly, this argument even received the endorsement of the World Bank in its 1987 *World Development Report*.
11. OECD, *Agricultural Policy Reform: Developments and prospects*, June 2000.
12. 'Failing farmers learn to profit from federal aid', *New York Times*, 24 December 2000.
13. 'Free market left Haiti's rice growers behind', *Washington Post*, 13 April 2000.
14. World Bank commodity price statistics.
15. 'Vietnam left with a bitter taste', *Observer*, 12 August 2001.
16. These conventions define standards in different areas of employment (e.g. trade union rights) which member states can adopt on a selective basis, thereby binding themselves to apply them.
17. Until then tax havens had been confined to a relatively small number of locations, mainly in Europe (e.g. the Channel Islands, Liechtenstein).
18. *Towards Global Tax Co-operation*, report to the 2000 Ministerial Council Meeting and recommendations by the Committee on Fiscal Affairs. See also *Harmful Tax Competition: An Emerging Global Issue*, OECD, 1998.
19. 'EU changes tax', *Financial Times*, 29 January 2001.
20. From figures cited (disapprovingly) in J. Bhagwati, 'A costly pursuit of free trade', *Financial Times*, 6 March 2001.

CHAPTER 5

1. Derived from statistical data in World Bank, *World Development Report 1982, 1996, 2000*. Although the calculations, which exclude data for the former centrally planned economies of the Soviet bloc, are evidently

subject to some margin of error, they may be taken as a valid indicator of the direction of change. It should be pointed out also that they overstate the difference in living standards substantially, mainly due to distorted exchange rates, although according to the most recent World Bank estimates based on 'purchasing power parity' the industrial market economies are still 7–8 times better off (estimates for earlier periods are not available).

2. International Monetary Fund, 'The world economy in the twentieth century: Striking developments and policy lessons', Chapter V of *World Economic Outlook*, May 2000.

3. Paul Rogers, *Losing Control: Global Security in the 21st Century*, Pluto Press, London, 2000.

4. World Bank, *World Development Report 1999/2000*, p. 30.

5. Cf. P.T. Bauer, *Dissent on Development: Studies and debates on development economics*, London, Weidenfeld & Nicolson, 1971.

6. US Congress, *Report of the International Financial Institution Advisory Commission* (the Meltzer Commission) March 2000.

7. The exceptions are mainly small enclaves such as Hong Kong and Macao, which have been absorbed into larger political entities from which they were originally excised.

8. Data source: World Bank, *World Development Report 1999/2000*.

9. The devastating impact, economic and social, of the declining viability of plantation agriculture had in fact been understood for decades, as revealed by successive Royal Commissions on the British West Indies, culminating in the report of the Moyne Commission of 1937–38 (HMSO, West India Royal Commission Report, Cmnd 6607, London, 1945).

10. Two notable examples are Papua New Guinea and Suriname, both granted political 'independence' in 1975 (by Australia and the Netherlands respectively).

11. Basil Davidson, *The Story of Africa*, London, Mitchell Beazley, 1984.

12. Notably in the many works of Noam Chomsky, including *Deterring Democracy*, London, Verso, 1991.

13. *North–South: A programme for survival*, Pan Books, London, 1980.

14. US Congress, *Report of the International Financial Institution Advisory Commission*.

15. It is also highly convenient in the context of its domestic agricultural policy, which (as noted in Chapter 4) still involves the accumulation of large stocks of grain and other foodstuffs that need to be disposed of without antagonizing its trading partners unduly.

16. Edberto M. Villegas, *Global Finance Capital and the Philippine Financial System*, Manila, Institute of Political Economy, 2000.

17. As the author has observed at first hand in sub-Saharan Africa and elsewhere.

18. *Financial Times*, 4 March 1997; 16 February 2001.

CHAPTER 6

1. This term is used to denote any body representative of the community, either at local, national or supranational level.
2. The first actual instance of this is the creation of Glas Cymru (a consortium of business, charities, local authorities and other public bodies) to take over the assets of Welsh Water in 2001.
3. Prompted mainly by growing concerns as to the desirability of large-scale factory farming in view of its possible impact on both animal and human health and welfare.
4. See 'Triumph of the suits', *FOMC Alert*, 21 December 1999. Financial Markets Center, Philomont, VA.
5. 'Yearning for stability spurs surge of regional harmony', *Financial Times*, 7 March 2001.

CHAPTER 7

1. The vote was 48-0, with only the Soviet republics and South Africa abstaining.
2. Broadly following those already enshrined in the Universal Declaration itself.
3. Some 153 out of 193 as of February 2001. The most significant exceptions are in Asia (Saudi Arabia and other Gulf states, Pakistan, Burma, Indonesia, Malaysia and Singapore).
4. The two cases are not entirely comparable, since whereas Kosovo was recognized by the UN as legally part of Yugoslavia, East Timor had never been recognized as part of Indonesia after the latter illegally invaded it in 1975, although this had been done with the tacit blessing of the United States.
5. Information Services Latin America, www.igc.org/isla, April 2001.
6. John Pilger, 'Phoney war', *Guardian*, 19 October 1999.
7. President Clinton's belated move to do so just before leaving office at the beginning of 2001 may be considered an empty gesture, since it does not bind either his successor or Congress, who are solidly opposed to ratification.
8. Cf. George Monbiot, 'Running the world without a mandate', *Guardian*, 22 June 2000.
9. *Guardian*, 20 March 2001.
10. *Globalization and Governance*, UN Millennium Report, April 2000.
11. Ibid.
12. Comprising all 10 countries of South East Asia.
13. Argentina, Brazil, Paraguay and Uruguay.
14. All of the 15 member states except Greece are classified by the World Bank as 'high income'.

CHAPTER 8

1. 'The Nader campaign and the future of U.S. left electoral politics', *Monthly Review*, February 2001.

2. Richard Lapper, 'Anger in the Andes', *Financial Times*, 26 April 2000.

3. *The State in a Changing World*, World Development Report 1997.

4. Notably such apostles of 'Asian values' as Lee Kuan Yew of Singapore (by now in any case a more or less developed state) and Mahathir Mohamed of Malaysia.

5. E.g. J. Kay, 'The stakeholder corporation', in G. Kelly, D.Kelly and A. Gamble, eds, *Stakeholder Capitalism*, Macmillan, London, 1997.

INDEX

Abacha, Sani (former president of Nigeria), 96
accountability, 20, 36, 46, 54, 55, 99, 115, 118, 142,153, 154, 159; democratic, 62, 100, 102, 104, 105, 125, 138, 139; corporate (*see also* corporate governance), 67, 118
accounting (*see also* intangibles), 34; false, 59
Afghanistan, 21; war (Russian), 13
Africa, 15, 89, 91, 98; conflict in, 21, 127; former French colonies, 94; regional integration, 124, 140; Southern, 1, 140; US disengagement, 44
agricultural revolution, 23
agriculture, 5, 35, 104; commodity markets, 115; economics of, 75; trade, 74–7; state intervention, 116
Algeria, 18, 137
American revolution, 7
Angola, 21
anti-trust regulation (*see* monopoly)
Argentina, 162, 168
armaments industry (*see* defence industry)
Asia, 15, 21, 25, 51, 52, 55, 89, 102; financial crisis, 2, 31, 39, 40, 77, 141; 'tiger' economies, 39, 72; regional integration, 124, 140, 143
Asian Monetary Fund, proposed, 141
asset values (*see also* financial markets),

31, 34, 57; intangible, 34, 108
Australasia, 146
Austria, 7
Austrian school of economists, 51

balance of power, 22
banking industry/sector (*see also* financial institutions), 31, 43, 52, 56, 57, 61, 88, 112, 117, 120; deregulation, 57, 121
Berlusconi, Silvio, 63
Beveridge Report, 163
Blair, Tony, 63
Bosnia, 130, 132
Brandt Commission on International Development, 98
Brazil, 162, 168
Britain, 6, 7, 9, 20, 29, 38, 44, 49, 51, 63, 72, 111, 112, 122; animal production, deregulation, 50; democracy in, 8, 45, 146, 148, 149; financial deregulation, 59; 'free' trade in, 72; imperial policy, 20, 37, 45, 95; labour regulation, reneges on ILO conventions, 79; pensions industry, 65; privatization experience, 65, 110, 111; 'social contract', 55; Third World dictators supported by, 94, 96; unemployment trends, 69–70
Brown, Gordon, 70
budgetary deficits (*see* fiscal deficits)
Buffet, Warren, 162
Burma, 29, 168
Bush, President George, 14, 18

150; financial crises, 31; military dictatorships, 14, 150; political instability, 21

Law, John, 60

League of Nations, 7–9, 139

'lender of last resort' (state as), 117

less developed countries (LDCs) (*see also* Third World), 86; inherent non-viability of, 91–3; leaders' lack of interest in promoting development, 101–2

Levitt, Arthur, 60, 165

liberalization (and deregulation), 31, 38, 39, 50, 57, 58, 76, 77–81, 88, 90, 107, 115; stimulus to economic crime, 43, 57–61, 80

Libya, 133

limited liability, 54, 110, 117, 153, 157

Malthus, T.R., 165

market demand, 26, 32, 34, 48; and excess supply capacity, 52

market distortions, 39, 49, 54, 57, 58, 65, 66, 68, 74–83, 90, 106, 112, 115, 119, 140, 156; buying back of shares, 31

market regulation, 47, 49, 50, 51, 60, 111–12, 115, 120, 124–5

mass media: influence of big business on, 2, 4, 56, 57, 63, 147; need to prevent control by sectional interests, 122, 157–8

'mercantilism', 72

MERCOSUR, 140

Metternich, 22

Mexico, 2, 21, 40, 43, 44, 77, 88, 89

Microsoft Corporation, 49, 54

Middle East, 1, 12; authoritarian governments, 18; US policy, 18, 99, 135

military–industrial complexes, 12, 25

Minow, N., 165

'minimalist' state, 150

Mobutu, President, 17, 96

monetary integration, 124, 140, 143

money laundering, reluctance of Bush administration to crack down, 61

Monks, R., 165

monopoly, 47, 49; restraints on (anti-trust), 49; natural, 51, 111

'moral hazard', 57–8, 65, 112, 117

Mullan, P., 163

Murdoch, Rupert, 63

Nader, Ralph, 149

Namibia, 21

neo-colonialism/neo-imperialism, 151

neo-liberalism (*see laissez faire*; 'free' markets)

'new economy', 2, 32, 36, 58

Nicaragua, 14, 96

Nkrumah, Kwame, 95

non-profit organisations, 118

North American Free Trade Association (NAFTA), 82

North Atlantic Treaty Organisation (NATO), 131

Novartis, 64

organized crime, 59, 61

OECD (Organization for Economic Cooperation and Development): countries, 27, 31, 66, 69, 70, 71, 75, 76, 78; attempts to limit tax competition, 80–1

offshore financial centres/tax havens, 61, 80

OPEC (Organization of Petroleum Exporting Countries), 88

Pakistan, 149, 168

Palestine question, 18

Panama, 14, 132

pension funds, 30, 60, 61, 117, 118; increasing fragility, 2, 28, 65, 118

Philippines, 7, 21; comprador bourgeoisie, 101

Pinochet (ex-president of Chile), 17

political parties, funding of, 62, 121–2, 147–9, 150, 157

political patronage, 122, 158–9

population growth, 5, 35, 71, 86, 87, 91, 107

power élite (*see* establishment, global/ruling)

predatory pricing, 48, 114

privatization, 29, 51, 110, 111, 112; failure of, 65

productivity (of capital and labour), 26, 71

THE GLOBAL ISSUES SERIES

Already available

Robert Ali Brac de la Perrière and Franck Seuret, *Brave New Seeds: The Threat of GM Crops to Farmers*

Oswaldo de Rivero, *The Myth of Development: The Non-viable Economies of the 21ᵗ Century*

Joyeeta Gupta, *Our Simmering Planet: What to do about Global Warming?*

Nicholas Guyatt, *Another American Century? The United States and the World after 2000*

Martin Khor, *Rethinking Globalization: Critical Issues and Policy Choices*

John Madeley, *Hungry for Trade: How the Poor Pay for Free Trade*

Riccardo Petrella, *The Water Manifesto: Arguments for a World Water Contract*

Vandana Shiva, *Protect or Plunder? Understanding Intellectual Property Rights*

Harry Shutt, *A New Democracy: Alternatives to a Bankrupt World Order*

In preparation

Peggy Antrobus and Gigi Francisco, *The Women's Movement Worldwide: Issues and Strategies for the New Century*

Amit Bhaduri and Deepak Nayyar, *Free Market Economics: The Intelligent Person's Guide to Liberalization*

Jonathan Bloch and Paul Todd, *Business as Usual? Intelligence Agencies and Secret Services in the New Century*

Julian Burger, *First Peoples: What Future?*

Richard Douthwaite, *Go for Growth? Poverty, the Environment and the Pros and Cons of Economic Growth*

Graham Dunkley, *Trading Development: Trade, Globalization and Alternative Development Possibilities*

John Howe, *A Ticket to Ride: Breaking the Transport Gridlock*

Calestous Juma, *The New Genetic Divide: Biotechnology in the Age of Globalization*

John Madeley, *Food for All: The Need for a New Agriculture*

Jeremy Seabrook, *The Future of Culture: Can Human Diversity Survive in a Globalized World?*

David Sogge, *Give and Take: What's the Matter with Foreign Aid?*

Keith Suter, *Curbing Corporate Power: How Can We Control Transnational Corporations?*

Oscar Ugarteche, *A Level Playing Field: Changing the Rules of the Global Economy*

Nedd Willard, *The Drugs War: Is This the Solution?*

For full details of this list and Zed's other subject and general catalogues, please write to: The Marketing Department, Zed Books, 7 Cynthia Street, London N1 9JF, UK or email Sales@zedbooks. demon.co.uk

Visit our website at: www.zedbooks.demon.co.uk

Participating Organizations

Both ENDS   A service and advocacy organization which collaborates with environment and indigenous organizations, both in the South and in the North, with the aim of helping to create and sustain a vigilant and effective environmental movement.

> Damrak 28-30, 1012 LJ Amsterdam, The Netherlands
> Phone: +31 20 623 0823   Fax: +31 20 620 8049
> Email: info@bothends.org
> Website: www.bothends.org

Catholic Institute for International Relations (CIIR)   CIIR aims to contribute to the eradication of poverty through a programme that combines advocacy at national and international level with community-based development.

> Unit 3, Canonbury Yard, 190a New North Road, London N1 7BJ, UK
> Phone +44 (0)20 7354 0883   Fax +44 (0)20 7359 0017
> Email: ciir@ciir.org
> Website: www.ciir.org

Corner House   The Corner House is a UK-based research and solidarity group working on social and environmental justice issues in North and South.

> PO Box 3137, Station Road, Sturminster Newton, Dorset DT10 1YJ, UK
> Tel.: +44 (0)1258 473795   Fax: +44 (0)1258 473748
> Email: cornerhouse@gn.apc.org
> Website: www.cornerhouse.icaap.org

Council on International and Public Affairs (CIPA)   CIPA is a human rights research, education and advocacy group, with a particular focus on economic and social rights in the USA and elsewhere around the world. Emphasis in recent years has been given to resistance to corporate domination.

> 777 United Nations Plaza, Suite 3C, New York, NY 10017, USA
> Tel. +1 212 972 9877   Fax +1 212 972 9878
> E-mail: cipany@igc.org
> Website: www.cipa-apex.org

Dag Hammarskjöld Foundation   The Dag Hammarskjöld Foundation, established 1962, organises seminars and workshops on social, economic and cultural issues facing developing countries with a particular focus on alternative and innovative solutions. Results are published in its journal *Develpment Dialogue*.

Övre Slottsgatan 2, 753 10 Uppsala, Sweden.
Tel.: +46 18 102772   Fax: +46 18 122072
e-mail: secretariat@dhf.uu.se
Website: www.dhf.uu.se

Development GAP   The Development Group for Alternative Policies
is a Non-Profit Development Resource Organization working with
popular organizations in the South and their Northern partners in support of a development that is truly sustainable and that advances social
justice.

927 15th Street NW, 4th Floor, Washington, DC, 20005, USA
Tel.: +1 202 898 1566   Fax: +1 202 898 1612
E-mail: dgap@igc.org
Website: www.developmentgap.org

Focus on the Global South   Focus is dedicated to regional and
global policy analysis and advocacy work. It works to strengthen the
capacity of organizations of the poor and marginalized people of the
South and to better analyse and understand the impacts of the globalization process on their daily lives.

C/o CUSRI, Chulalongkorn University, Bangkok 10330, Thailand
Tel.: +66 2 218 7363 Fax: +66 2 255 9976
Email: Admin@focusweb.org
Website: www.focusweb.org

Inter Pares   Inter Pares, a Canadian social justice organization, has
been active since 1975 in building relationships with Third World
development groups and providing support for community-based
development programs. Inter Pares is also involved in education and
advocacy in Canada, promoting understanding about the causes, effects
and solutions to poverty.

58 rue Arthur Street, Ottawa, Ontario, KIR 7B9 Canada
Phone +1 613 563 4801   Fax +1 613 594 4704

Public Interest Research Centre   PIRC is a research and campaigning group based in Delhi which seeks to serve the information needs of
activists and organizations working on macro-economic issues concerning finance, trade and development.

142 Maitri Apartments, Plot No. 28, Patparganj, Delhi 110092, India
Phone: +91 11 2221081/2432054   Fax: +91 11 2224233
Email: kaval@nde.vsnl.net.in

Third World Network   TWN is an international network of groups and individuals involved in efforts to bring about a greater articulation of the needs and rights of peoples in the Third World; a fair distribution of the world's resources; and forms of development which are ecologically sustainable and fulfil human needs. Its international secretariat is based in Penang, Malaysia.

228 Macalister Road, 10400 Penang, Malaysia
Tel.: +60 4 226 6159   Fax: +60 4 226 4505
Email: twnet@po.jaring.my
Website: www.twnside.org.sg

Third World Network–Africa   TWN–Africa is engaged in research and advocacy on economic, environmental and gender issues. In relation to its current particular interest in globalization and Africa, its work focuses on trade and investment, the extractive sectors and gender and economic reform.

2 Ollenu Street, East Legon, PO Box AN19452, Accra-North, Ghana.
Tel.: +233 21 511189/503669/500419   Fax: +233 21 511188
email: twnafrica@ghana.com

World Development Movement (WDM)   The World Development Movement campaigns to tackle the causes of poverty and injustice. It is a democratic membership movement that works with partners in the South to cancel unpayable debt and break the ties of IMF conditionality, for fairer trade and investment rules, and for strong international rules on multinationals.

25 Beehive Place, London SW9 7QR, UK
Tel.: +44 (0)20 7737 6215   Fax: +44 (0)20 7274 8232
E-mail: wdm@wdm.org.uk
Website: www.wdm.org.uk

THIS BOOK IS ALSO AVAILABLE
IN THE FOLLOWING COUNTRIES

EGYPT

MERIC
(The Middle East Readers'
Information Center)
2 Bahgat Ali Street,
Tower D/Apt. 24
Zamalek
Cairo
Tel: 20 2 735 3818/736 3824
Fax: 20 2 736 9355

FIJI

University Book Centre,
University of South Pacific,
Suva
Tel: 679 313 900
Fax: 679 303 265

GHANA

EPP Book Services,
PO Box TF 490,
Trade Fair,
Accra
Tel: 233 21 778347
Fax: 233 21 779099

MOZAMBIQUE

Sul Sensações
PO Box 2242,
Maputo
Tel: 258 1 421974
Fax: 258 1 423414

NAMIBIA

Book Den
PO Box 3469
Shop 4, Frans Indongo Gardens
Windhoek
Tel: 264 61 239976
Fax: 264 61 234248

NEPAL

Everest Media Services,
GPO Box 5443, Dillibazar
Putalisadak Chowk

Kathmandu
Tel: 977 1 416026
Fax: 977 1 250176

PAPUA NEW GUINEA

Unisearch PNG Pty Ltd
Box 320, University
National Capital District
Tel: 675 326 0130
Fax: 675 326 0127

RWANDA

Librairie Ikirezi
PO Box 443
Kigali
Tel/Fax: 250 71314

SUDAN

The Nile Bookshop
New Extension Street 41
P O Box 8036
Khartoum
Tel: 249 11 463749

TANZANIA

TEMA Publishing Co Ltd
PO Box 63115
Dar Es Salaam
Tel: 255 22 2113608
Fax: 255 22 2110472

UGANDA

Aristoc Booklex Ltd
PO Box 5130, Kampala Road
Diamond Trust Building
Kampala
Tel: 256 41 344381/349052
Fax: 256 41 254867

ZAMBIA

UNZA Press
PO Box 32379
Lusaka
Tel: 260 1 290409
Fax: 260 1 253952

www.ingramcontent.com/pod-product-compliance
Ingram Content Group UK Ltd.
Pitfield, Milton Keynes, MK11 3LW, UK
UKHW031253020325
455690UK00007B/57